Discovering Your Unique
God-Designed Rhythm

Tami J Gray

Copyright © 2024 by Tami J Gray

Fearlessly Unbecoming
Published by Kennimer Publishing
PO Box 241
Gilmer, TX 75644
www.tamijgray.com

All rights reserved. No part of this publication may be reproduced, distributed, or transmitted in any form or by any means, including photocopying, recording, or other electronic or mechanical methods, without the prior written permission of the publisher, except in the case of brief quotations embodied in critical reviews and certain other noncommercial uses permitted by copyright law. For permission requests, write to the publisher, addressed 'Attention: Permissions Coordinator,' at the address above.

All Scripture quotations, unless otherwise indicated, are taken from the Holy Bible, New International Version®, NIV®. Copyright ©1973, 1978, 1984, 2011 by Biblica, Inc.™ Used by permission of Zondervan. All rights reserved worldwide. www.zondervan.com. The "NIV" and "New International Version" are trademarks registered in the United States Patent and Trademark Office by Biblica, Inc.™

The author has added italics to Scripture quotations for emphasis.

ISBN 979-8-218-44904-9 (paperback)
eISBN 979-8-218-44905-6 (epub)

Library of Congress Control Number: 2024924540

Cover design by Shonda Ramsey
Edited by TJ Ray and Niki Banning

Printed in the United States of America
First Edition 2024

10 9 8 7 6 5 4 3 2 1

121124

Endorsements

"If you've ever been the girl-woman lying in a heap on the floor, wounded and broken, then *Fearlessly Unbecoming* is the book for you. This book has helped me to finally understand the difference between living as a "Christian good girl," at which I was **never** successful, and living as – *being* – a beloved daughter of the Most High King. *Fearlessly Unbecoming* is based solidly on Scripture, prayer, and the incredibly vulnerable honesty of the author. That combination is what drew me deeper into the book.

I finally understand – and believe – how much my King loves this particular daughter."

—Shelby DellaRosa
Author of *Going Up to Jerusalem: A Story of Becoming*
Launch Strategist for Christian Coaches

"*Fearlessly Unbecoming* by Tami J Gray is a genuine and heartfelt guide to living out authentic faith. Tami's honest reflections and practical insights—*like choosing to walk to Jesus, seeing our words as arrows, and understanding that God never moves away from us*—made this book relatable and encouraging. *Fearlessly Unbecoming* is perfect for anyone looking to deepen their walk with Christ in a real and meaningful way."

—Shonda Ramsey
Author of *Authentically Anchored*
Book and Brand Designer for Authors and Entrepreneurs

"As Tami J Gray's editor, I've had a unique perspective of her beautiful book, *Fearlessly Unbecoming*. And I have been blessed because of it. Tami's book drew me in from the start. With her vulnerable sharing, insights, and encouragement to dig deeper into God's Word, she brings you into her world and shares her heart for learning to accept your place at His table. Whether you're a dress-wearing or Converse-sporting kind of gal, Tami's book will inspire you to receive His love for you, right where you are."

–Niki Banning
Story Guardian for Christian Authors
nikibvirtualservices.com

Dedication

for the King of Kings, with deepest gratitude & reverence

Contents

Endorsements

Dedication

Introduction

How to Engage While Reading

Letter to My Younger Self

Section 1: The Unlikely Heiress

    Chapter 1 21

    Chapter 2 35

    Chapter 3 47

Section 1 Scripture Reading 61

Section 2: The Battlefield

    Chapter 4 67

    Chapter 5 79

    Chapter 6 91

Section 2 Scripture Reading 103

Letter to My Younger Self 105

Section 3: Mermaids Don't Dog Paddle

    Chapter 7 109

    Chapter 8 121

    Chapter 9 133

Section 3 Scripture Reading 143

Conclusion 147

Acknowledgements 149

About the Author 153

Introduction

At 36, my second husband and I got married. He offered me the choice of beautiful wedding rings. But I insisted on tattooed wedding rings instead. We had both been through previous marriages, and I knew–come what may–this was it for me. It was not a decision I made lightly, and I had no intention of giving up on it. Little did I know what life would bring in the 14 years we have been married. I don't know how, but we were still naïve, even in our mid-thirties with multiple marriages between us.

As a teen, I assumed my thirties would come with wisdom and a solid foundation on which to live the rest of my life. I never imagined my first marriage would crumble and I would begin a new life as a single mother. My plans were to be happily married, living my dream as a sweet little family with a house full of kids.

Insert my good little Christian girl mentality. Living as a mom and wife, I attempted to play the parts of each well. I did the crafts, read the Bible Studies, took part in the church activities, and more. I grew up believing this is what adulthood looked like. Eventually, I crashed hard. Teenage depression turned into postpartum depression, and behaving as I thought others wanted turned into anxiety. Many days, anxiety stopped me in my tracks. On other days, I tried to keep up the appearance of a good Christian, but without realizing it, I was failing miserably. I thought everyone was acting their way through life, expecting Oscar-worthy performances from me as well. Turns out, they weren't.

The people around me lived authentically while dealing with their traumas, hurts, and hang-ups. My false sense of righteousness, mixed with the struggles we all deal with independently, created a toxic cocktail that led to many relationships, including my first marriage, disintegrating. I soon realized how difficult relationships of any kind can be. I adopted the phrase, "Relationships are less about making me happy and more about making me holy."

Seeing each relationship I am blessed with as they truly are–flawed people falling down and getting back up–while hopefully doing as little damage as possible to ourselves and others. It took me well into my thirties to learn that lesson–and I can confidently say I am still learning it. Having tattooed wedding rings helped solidify a new relationship and held it together through heavy times that we were not sure we would survive.

Those little reminders, permanently placed on our ring fingers, cannot be dramatically taken off and thrown across the room while slamming the door behind in the heat of the moment. The permanence has meant we must think twice about saying words we cannot take back through all: turmoil, joy, death, celebration–and lots of whiskey prayers. Each crazy, painful, beautiful experience brought me to my knees, even if at times in a haze. Many times, I imagined laying my head on the lap of the Father, pouring my weary soul out to Him, as He gently patted my head and lovingly spoke life back into me.

While I write this book, in a way to my past self, I hope it meets you where you are and helps you glide over the obstacles I tripped, sloshed, rolled, and wallowed in through the years.

In the middle of dating and subsequently marrying my current husband, I heard God say, "Write." No details, just one word. I did not know if He meant a book, a story, a song, a letter, a blog, or something else entirely. Turns out, I've dabbled in almost all of those things, but never quite settled on any one. But I knew He said, "Write," and it was unmistakably His voice. It is hard to explain; I simply knew.

Months later, as I was in the passenger seat of my husband's beat-up old truck on the way to church one Sunday morning, I heard, *"Tattooed Wedding Rings & Whiskey Prayers."* I immediately knew these words were the title of–well, whatever I would write. At the time I am writing this book, you can still find a blog under that title because there have been fits and starts all these many years of practicing writing, and that title has been consistent in its surety and connectedness, while my writing was not.

As a matter of fact, this book began with that exact title because it is so fitting for so many readers–myself included. Depending on where you are in life, the title could just as easily be called *"Single Parent & Tears in the Pillow"* or maybe *"Bury Your Head and Stuff Your Feelings in Food"* (this hits close to home for sure). *"Workaholic & Too Many Pills?"* or *"Put a Smile On, Pretending Everything is Okay."* However you choose to hide, it is all the same concept. We cling to tiny glimmers of hope in difficult times–hoping we will come out on the other side. We are not always asking to come out on the other side better. Sometimes, just getting through is the best we can hope for. And that is okay.

After completing the writing of this book, as it was in editing and cover design, we realized that *Tattooed Wedding Rings & Whiskey*

INTRODUCTION | 11

Prayers was no longer the title for this book. The book had become about all that had to be undone within me through the years. All the false beliefs and expectations which had to be shed to get back to who I was created to be. I am absolutely not who I once was–and I barely recognize that girl or young mom anymore. Each season has been about letting go of more. Many seasons, like the death of my parents, I did not believe I would survive. Yet even that season brought more to shed and brought me closer to myself and to God.

Fearlessly Unbecoming describes how and why I had to shed so much in order to find myself. It describes my misunderstandings and misjudgments that led me to spend years trying to live a life of someone who doesn't even exist - and was never meant to. Come to think of it, I may actually spend the rest of my life unbecoming that person. Maybe that is what the second half of life is really about. Undoing the facade you spent the first half of your life building. I keep saying I feel the most like myself with purple hair and tattoos. While I don't always have purple hair, the tattoos are permanent reminders to myself of who I am at my core. After years of trying to be a good little Christian girl, I took (what some call) drastic steps to make sure she never came back. I realized I could never be her and she was no longer welcome within me. I can't pretend. Pretending is not an option, and having tattoos allowed me the freedom to quit doing just that. I do not want to hide or pretend any longer. I never was that person–and it is ok to live as myself.

Of course, that is not the answer for everyone and was not the only answer for me, but it is the choice I made and I am glad I did. There is not one ounce of me that scares God away or makes Him consider me unloveable. I will not join the debate on whether tattoos are acceptable to Him or not because *I* am acceptable to Him. You are acceptable to Him. While religion may dismiss you based on looks, He will not. So, let's be fearless together, unbecome all that we *thought* we should be, and learn for ourselves who we are.

I've come too far to give you the cliche line that I will be right there "in the mud" with you. I cannot know your exact situation, but I still get stuck in the mud plenty, so I understand how being in that muck feels.

There are three quotes I have come to love through this season:

1. *"We are all just walking each other home."* [1]
2. *"I may not jump in the ocean to drown with you, but you are welcome in my boat anytime."* [2]
3. *"There is someone that I love even though I don't approve of what he does. There is someone I accept though some of his thoughts and actions revolt me. There is someone I forgive though he hurts the people I love the most. That person is......me"* [3]

For me, each of these quotes tells a story of hope. Not a life of glamour or ease, but hope in Him and those He uses to help pull us out of the deep end. My goal for this book is to take your hand, help you navigate where I've been, and keep moving forward together to Him–toward Home.

Each section in *Fearlessly Unbecoming* is based on a challenging yet beautiful lesson I had to learn. I pray my lessons give you the roadmap to avoid as many hazards as possible.

Be sweet to yourself, but do the hard work.

tjg

How to Engage While Reading

You will notice many intentional pauses throughout the book. These pauses are there for a few reasons.

1. The pauses are there to help you stop and think about the topics we are discussing. Write them down in a journal or simply spend a few moments asking God to discuss them with you. I encourage you to spend some time with them. To make the greatest impact, it is important to read expecting to have our hearts touched by Him.

2. I have designed the book with you in mind. You do not need to power through an entire chapter in one sitting. Sometimes, when needed, simmer on what you read for a while. It could be a few moments or even a few days. Life happens- laundry, busy days, or only five minutes to spare. If you need to stop reading, stop. No expectations, no guilt. Consider this your friendly reminder that God is not expecting long hours of focused time, and He is not mad at you. If you give Him five minutes of intentional time, He cherishes it and meets you there! No one is testing you on the contents you read. It is for your benefit–not obligation.

3. I have concluded each chapter with a poetic summation, which is a creative expression of God's love for us. As a young girl, one of my favorite books was *The Tales of the Kingdom*, by David and Karen Maines. In this book of fairytale stories, with a Christian emphasis, the authors end each chapter with a summary of the lesson learned by the characters. Those few sentences captured my attention and drove home the lifeblood of each chapter. God used them to inspire my writing style of throwing in a tiny fairytale anywhere I can. I take the visual beauty He reveals to me and blend it with the harsh contrast of black and white letters on a page. Together, the two make beautiful illustrations that you can only view with the mind's eye and that only He can inspire. Oh, how I wish I could create visual art from the images He shows me, but painting with words is what I have and I hope to glorify Him and do His visuals justice with the words I whimsically weave in storybook fashion. I hope their juxtaposition to the chapter will cause them to jump off the page and show you a picture of yourself, as a royal relation to The King, being held, taught, and loved by Him.

This is *your* journey with God; He is never in a rush—He simply enjoys spending time with you.

A Letter To The Princess Who Lost Her Crown

Hey you. Well, me—younger me, I guess I should say.

First, I need you to know that you are okay—We are okay. We are still here, so for that, I want to say "Thank you." It means we can try again; if we fail, get up and try again. Thank you for being brave enough to keep going. All because you were fearless enough to stay. Time is the gift you have given to me. In return, I offer you the gifts of forgiveness, acceptance, love, and wisdom.

Thank you for moving forward, even when you feel you aren't.

I forgive you for assuming you are not enough. *You are enough. Exactly who and how you are.*

I know you struggle to love yourself, so I offer you the love you deserve. You are worthy simply because He says you are.

Throughout your life, Dad repeatedly told you to "be sweet." He felt you were too harsh, too negative, and too unfriendly. In reality, you were too self-condemning and carried too much pressure. You felt the world's weight on your shoulders from a young age—which certainly did not soften your rough edges. You used to say if you ever wrote a book, it would be called *"The Porcupine Wearing a Barbed Wire Coat Who Needs a Hug."* The need to soften and let your guard down was a longing, but the reality of it did not come until much later in life. For too many years, that barbed wire coat was used to protect yourself from all the pain and heaviness you carried.

You waited way too long to take that coat off and allow yourself to relax. To love and be loved. You learned the protection put up was not only keeping you from being hurt, but it also kept you from appearing lovable and able to love. It is time to quit hibernating in that barbed wire coat.

Over the years, I have learned that accepting myself for who I am makes it much easier to accept those around me unconditionally.

So this book is for you. I wish I had learned all of this sooner so I could have protected the little girl you were, the scared and self-loathing teenager, and the young woman who would have done almost anything for the love she desperately thought she needed from others.

There are two types of love you and I needed. Most importantly, we needed the love of God. He has been the unwavering pillar of stability throughout all the ages and stages we've experienced. Second, I needed you to love yourself. You couldn't see that, and I forgive you. We have worked hard to find a place where we can love ourselves. With those two forms of love, the rest is coming together–finally. I can finally begin giving the love we did not know how to give and receiving the love we did not know how to receive. Now, our journey together can be exciting and fulfilling.

We are okay.
I forgive you and love you.
Be sweet to yourself.

Section 1:

The Unlikely Heiress

Chapter 1

You Are More Than You Realize

"Now if we are children, then we are heirs—heirs of God and co-heirs with Christ, if indeed we share in his sufferings in order that we may also share in his glory."—Romans 8:17 (NIV)[4]

    I pretty much grew up in the church, constantly striving to be that perfect Christian girl I believed everyone expected me to be. You know the type—cute dresses, hair with curls, and a perpetual smile. The girl who never questions authority, responds with a "yes ma'am," and carefully handles the "no ma'am" situations. She can quote scripture, dive into all the church activities, volunteer for anything, and proudly tote her Bible to school, spreading the love of Jesus to everyone. You likely have your own idea of an ideal Christian girl, and believe me–I would have tried to fit it.

    I failed mostly, but that did not keep me from trying and beating myself up when I failed. These girls, who are shown to be perfect, become the standard of behavior. But I knew inside I could never measure up. Deep down, I longed to be the good Christian girl I imagined. I also longed for something different which led me to believe there must be something wrong with me. At a very young age, expectations versus reality began a war within me. And I did not know how to stop it.

I began realizing the depths of this war as a young married mom with a little girl under the age of eight. I would love to say I was doing all I could to show up for my husband and daughter as the woman of God I believed I should be. Honestly, I had wasted much of my life pursuing happiness in the wrong ways and places, rebelling against constant admonishments to "straighten up and act right." As a young mom, this war was raging hard and it was about to come to a head.

One particular day all my acting crumbled completely. My daughter was spending the night with my parents since I had determined today was the day I would figure out what my gut had been trying to tell me for so long. And find out, I did. Remember the saying, "Be careful what you ask for?" At this moment, it is more true than ever. Full of turmoil, some simmering under the surface and some parading out in broad daylight, my inner unrest finally hit its breaking point, like a volcano after lying dormant for many years. And my marriage would never recover from the news I discovered that day (although at the time I was still naïve and hopeful).

I, without realizing, collapsed from the weight of truth too heavy to hold, curled up in the fetal position, crying. Experiencing a level of devastation I had never known, I was on the ground crying out to God, convinced I would not survive. The hurt was too much. This hopelessness felt insurmountable.

My legs went limp, and I could not catch myself as I fell. Realizing I was laying on our beige, uncomfortable Berber carpet, I felt as if I would simply melt into the floor and dissolve into a puddle of tears, leaving behind only a faint memory of a woman, a wife, a mom. Getting up was not an option. I didn't choose to lie down. My body refused to hold the weight of my heart and soul.

I felt as if I couldn't breathe, gasping for breath and crying out to God. I felt wounded and shattered. But in that moment, God ever so gently looked out and saw His hurting child, curled up like an infant scrunched inside its mother's womb. The only difference between a preborn infant and me at that moment was hope and fight.

And I had neither.

An infant fights through the muck and comes out screaming. But I resigned to lie in it, believing there was no other choice.

Pause and Ponder

Do you remember a moment when you received devastating news? What situation in your life comes to mind similar to mine? May I speak some truth into your life right now? Sister, you have survived. The situation may seem bleak, but the story is still being written. Trust me, good news is on the way.

What thoughts about your situation, and yourself, come up?

- Did you feel inadequate, unloved, unwanted, fearful, or something else?
- Please permit yourself to feel. Your valid feelings deserve a moment's reflection. Remind yourself that you will not stay here. Remember, good news is on the way.
- Can you relate to growing up with similar feelings to me about Christianity?

YOU ARE MORE THAN YOU REALIZE | 23

- What expectations do you recall being placed on you that seemed unattainable?
- Did you find you gave up and acted out because you couldn't meet their version of "good" you thought was expected?
- Or did you internalize every discrepancy, assuming something was wrong with you, as I did?

I encourage you to jot down the expectations you thought of. I hope that by the end of this book, you can glance back on your list and recognize the lies you believed instead of seeing them as failures.

I Heard Him say, "Then Get Up."

Time seemed to freeze. I assumed I was on the floor for eternity, but God had only given me a few moments to wallow in sorrow. Quickly, a booming yet calm voice asks within me; ***"Is this how a child of Mine behaves?"*** It was distinct and commanding, yet soothingly gentle. Before I had time to think, I responded with "No, sir."

"Then get up," He directed softly yet fiercely. I slowly pulled myself to a sitting position before finally standing up, taking a few breaths, and calming slightly.

Somewhere within the depths of my soul, I knew life would go on. Leaning against Him was my only option now. But honestly, I guess I can't say I *knew*. I *hoped*. Outwardly, I was not ready to believe yet. I hoped the times I heard others say–and even said myself, "We can depend on Him," "God is bigger than fears," and "Just have faith" were not empty cliches. Hope was all I had at this moment, however small it was. So I clung to hope. I could have stayed in that puddle, melting away with all the hurts of this world, but He had other plans. I knew enough from my years in church to trust and obey Him.

Suck It Up, Buttercup.

In the middle of that utter devastation, I had an experience with God that challenged and pivoted my relationship with Him forever. For several years now, a popular phrase has been "straighten your crown." This time of my life happened before this phrase was popular because I knew nothing about thinking of myself as a princess or royalty or anything more than what I had always been: plain, indistinct, unimportant, depressed, fearful, and feeling unwanted.

Over the next few weeks, after standing up out of despair and choosing to lean on Him, God began showing me who I was to Him. His child. His heir. While He did not specifically say, "Suck it up, Buttercup," I did not miss the uncanny similarities between what He was teaching me and all the times I used that phrase with my daughter. Let's just say I was not winning any awards for tender, loving mom of the year. While I was tender and loving in my feelings for people, I did not appear to be outwardly. As only God can do, He met me where I was and allowed me to learn in ways I understood. He was firm yet loving. He was unwavering in showing who He said I was compared to how I was acting.

"And so we know and rely on the love God has for us. God is love. Whoever lives in love lives in God, and God in them."—1 John 4:16 (NIV)[5]

God was taking me through hard lessons, yet simultaneously showing me the gentle and kind part of His love. He took me on a journey of learning what He meant when He referred to me as an heir.

I had never considered what being a child of God meant. I always understood it to mean "being saved" (believing Jesus died for our sins, asking for repentance, and choosing to follow His teachings). All of which I had done as a young girl, attending a tiny country church.

Wow. I was sadly shortsighted!

Yes, "being saved" is the beginning of our life as a Christian, , but what next? What about the rest of my life after I made such a choice? I spent all that time trying to be perfect, as I thought was expected. And I failed miserably. But I determined it was the only option I had. If you feel the expectation to be perfect and fail at it every single day, it can cause you to feel disappointed in yourself. For me, I grew up believing all the adults in my life were disappointed in me. Soon, I believed that God Himself found me to be a disappointment as well because I failed at being the perfect child He deserved. **I was so far off track.**

Pause and Ponder

- What are your thoughts about being God's child?
- Can you picture yourself as royalty? Not in a costume, but you, as you are, as royalty?
- Does this feel like a ridiculous thought or does it come easily?

Being saved is more than the cliche it can sound like at times. Being saved is the truth we experience when He lovingly pulls us up from the despair and darkness. He rescues us from the fear and loneliness, and the hate and self-loathing. He comes as a gentle warrior to scoop us up, defeat the darkness, and adopt us as His own. It is not a cliche. It is a rescue.

Acting like a Good Christian Girl Is a Joke.

Okay, hear me out. Yes, we should try to improve ourselves. Yes, we should focus on following God's Word and being Christ-like, but sometimes society teaches us that prioritizing "goodness" by its standards is the most important thing we should do.

It is not. Following worldly, or even religious standards of "goodness" may make us likable and compliant, but it is unrelated to being Christ-like. We should always find our guidance in Scripture, which teaches us what it means to be Christ-like. No matter who is teaching, we must be able to confirm their words in scripture. I hope you gain an understanding of what it means to be His heir while reading this book–through searching scripture for yourself and through prayer

"No man knows how bad he is till he has tried very hard to be good."
—CS Lewis[6]

I acted as if I believed everything I had been taught about being a Christian–but it was only an act. I acted as expectations demanded, yet I did not know what it meant or why I was doing it. I had read a lot of scripture, yet somehow never made the genuine connection until He showed me new ideas, beliefs, and old Biblical truths in new ways. I soaked it up because this was what a relationship with God should be! As God took me on a journey, I began seeing how a Christian truly should show up in life. I learned not about who others (or even I) believed I was–but of who He said I was, of who He is, and who YOU are.

Being His child is wildly beautiful!

God began having scriptures show up in different ways in my life. People would share them with me, or I would read a scripture and it would suddenly make sense as it never had before. Scriptures like the one my dad shared with me,

"...and if children, then heirs—heirs of God and joint heirs with Christ, if indeed we suffer with Him, that we may also be glorified together."
—Romans 8:17 (NKJV)[7]

Dictionary.com gives us these definitions, "***Joint***, adjective; Shared by or common to two or more. ***Heir***, noun; A person who inherits or is entitled to inherit the rank, title, positions, etc. of another."

Reading the scripture and understanding the meaning of the words, I considered the true meaning of being a princess again. I always imagined a princess living in a foreign country with rich family heritage, wealth, and privilege. Then, of course, were the fairytales. I loved them, but could never relate to those princesses because they were beautiful and graceful. I did not fit such a mold.

So I kept thinking, reading, and praying. If I was to believe what scripture was saying, it meant I was an adopted daughter of God. I am an equal heir to Christ, meaning God offers me an equal inheritance with Jesus. Yes, I understand Jesus is Jesus, and I am not. Jesus is Jesus, with all that comes with being the perfect Son of God. But, I imagine God looking at us and encouraging us with words like, "Come here, My child, and sit with Me just as Jesus would. Let Me love you and care for you as I do for Him." I had a hard time wrapping my brain around this concept, but He came through and helped me find a better understanding while prompting me to think about all scripture had to offer on the subject of being His child.

He also encouraged me to "Remember all those princess movies and books you have always loved. Do you remember how immensely the kings love the princesses and to what lengths they will go to protect their daughters?"

I began thinking about these questions frequently, and I would encourage you to do the same. Before you read any more of this book, think of all the movies you have seen or books you have read. See what ideas you can come up with about how people treat princesses–protect them, and provide for them. Take your time. This will still be here when you get back.

Pause and Ponder

- How do you perceive royalty to be treated?
- Which is your favorite princess from any movie, story, or song? And why?
- In what ways do you wish your life resembled a member of a royal family?
- Can you think of three things you have believed God thinks about you–which you now realize may not be true?

Father, I ask Your forgiveness for not realizing who You say I am sooner. I ask humbly that You awaken within me the desire to be who You created me to be. Revive the dreams You gave me long ago, even if I do not remember them, or please place new dreams inside me. I ask for You to show me who I am to You. Considering myself royalty will seem out of place some days because, as I look around me, I do not see the setting for royal life. On those days, I ask You to remind me Whose I am and how being royal has nothing to do with me–but everything to do with the fact that I am Your daughter. Only because You adopted me do I have access to being royal. Help me forgive myself and others who have not seen me as I am to You. Thank You for accepting me, even though I am only a ragamuffin trying to fit into Your royal family.

In the name of Your Son, Jesus Christ, Amen.

Learning who she was, she crawled out of the puddle, realizing her ballgown, drenched from tears, appeared dingy from her physical sorrow. Still, she leaned on the King for her strength, soaking up all the love and protection He offered. Then, slowly learning to stand again and hold her head a bit higher, she found the crown she had long since forgotten. It now graced her head as she forged a new determined path for only one thing. Eyes on Him. To this day, she is still learning who she is in her Father's kingdom. Maybe in step with her, we can let go of who others say we are, or how we label ourselves and journey hand in hand all the way home. To The King.

Chapter 2

Simmer In It

"If you, then, though you are evil, know how to give good gifts to your children, how much more will your Father in heaven give good gifts to those who ask him!"—Matthew 7:11 (NIV)[8]

I'm glad you're back. No, I am not being sarcastic. When reading a challenging book that causes me to look deep within or contemplate, it is easy to put the book down and not pick it back up. Doing so would be the easier choice, wouldn't it? I want to encourage you–if you stick it out, you will be grateful for this journey. While writing this book, I went back-and-forth feeling like I did not have the knowledge or time to complete it. One day, I felt a gentle whisper in my head say, "It is not about finding the time, but about offering the space." This idea essentially meant there would always be a reason I do not have the time, but if I change my perspective and think of it as an offering of time to Him instead, I would see the importance more vividly.

I do not want to steal from God by using the excuse of having other things to focus on. What could be more important than giving time for Him to inspire me and to do what He has instructed me to do? It reminds me of Genesis, where it says Adam walked with God in The Garden. I imagine them walking side by side, discussing fascinating topics, and even laughing together. That is the relationship I want. I have found that intentionally setting aside time for Him creates a close relationship that I have encountered nowhere else. We must not get tripped up believing our time has to look a certain way or have a particular agenda for Him to be there with us.

Should we spend it praying or standing with hands raised high in worship? Should we spend it reading or in quiet meditation? What if we do not have a full hour in our day to give Him? Friend, do not let the ideas someone else has placed in your head keep you from offering your time to God. You showing up is the right way. Some people play worship music and soak in the lyrics. Others pray or read the Bible. Others take time to rest their minds and bodies while thinking about focusing on what they know to be true about Him. Decide how and when you feel closest to God, and put those things into practice. If unsure, try different ways each time until you are sure.

I think of it like a little girl running up to her daddy to talk to him. Sometimes, she sadly curls up in his lap to cry as he listens and wipes her tears. Sometimes, she runs in and interrupts what he is doing with her excitement to tell him about something that has happened. Other times, she sheepishly comes in, needing to ask for forgiveness for something she has done. None of it is more correct than another. Each day brings challenges, wins, disappointments, or excitement. Each is okay. Offer the time, and as in any other relationship, the more you spend time with Him, the more He will share with you what He hopes your time together will be.

Pause and Ponder

- Do you want to give up when confronting complex spiritual topics?
- Are you willing to challenge yourself to keep going this time?
- How do you most frequently approach God?
- Do you avoid prayer or Bible study because you think you can never do it perfectly or up to the expectations of others?

When we experience unrealistic expectations, it sets us up for failure. Study your spiritual habits and see if you are holding yourself to a level that is not a good fit for you right now. An example of this is a new mom believing she must spend an hour every morning in prayer and reading her Bible. In some situations, this could be possible, but most situations would make this unattainable. Setting unrealistic expectations for yourself could happen because of what you have learned from others or because of assumptions you have made. Either way, determine now to accept the grace He offers that you have been ignoring because you did not believe it was for you. Decide that, for this week, you will spend time praying, reading, or whatever your next step needs to be. Be encouraged knowing five minutes is acceptable. Set a logical time limit for yourself and decide it is enough, even if it is not where you want to be. You are enough exactly where you are, and you will naturally grow.

Okay, back to where we left off in Chapter One:

Did you develop some ideas about how kings in fairy tales treat their princesses? Was thinking about the lives of royalty difficult? Some of it was for me because I was in the most brutal struggle of my life, and I felt as if focusing on pampered women was hurtful. They led a life of ease and protection, being desired and loved. Oh, of course, I know there is always a portion of the story where they have to suffer a loss or a hardship but come on, they usually have someone waiting to clean it up or offer them a nice warm bath and cozy bed to rest their weary heads. It was a challenging process, but I went through it because I knew it was necessary. As I forced myself to focus on it, the thoughts that came to my mind about it were:

- It doesn't matter if the princess in the story is sweet and kind or disobedient and outspoken. The running theme is that the king loved his daughter and would go to any length to protect her from whatever or whomever was out to harm her.
- I began thinking of how wars would rage at the thought of one princess being harmed or disrespected.
- I thought about how people lavish gifts and love upon a princess, even if those gifts are undeserved. How often do we see even a hateful, corrupt royal woman lavished in adoration?
- A princess receives the best education and training to help her prepare for what her life will entail.
- All those around a princess, respect the princess.
- A princess has nothing to fear because the king has himself and others constantly looking out for and protecting her.

- Most were naïve to actions taken behind the scenes for their benefit. People assigned to ensure she was okay, even when she had no idea they were doing it.

Did we come up with some of the same thoughts?

Please consider how important a royal woman is to her father and how respected she is. Again, I know not all stories are this way, but we will focus on those that are because they are examples of our story. **It is my story, and it is your story...**or it will be soon. So, friend, I encourage you to look in the mirror and imagine a crown sitting on your head or even buy yourself a real one to set out to remind you of who you are. I mean, you could go as far as I did and have one tattooed on, but I think it is safe to assume this is not the path for everyone.

- Is protection a topic that came up as you were thinking?
- Would you love to have the protection offered to royals?
- What about loyalty? Do you have loyal people in your relationships now, or is it a foreign idea?
- What is one thing royals have access to that you wish you could?

Holding my head a bit higher.

As the days progressed, I was thankful for the distractions and the reminders that kept coming as I collected these thoughts and ideas about being a princess. At some point, I felt God telling me, "Now take all those ideas and understand I would do all these things and more for you." What a foreign thought to me! I grew up with strong men in my family, and I knew they would do anything to protect me if there was

SIMMER IN IT | 37

a physical threat. Yet–emotions? Mental well-being? My heart? They didn't know how to handle those things well, so I learned to handle them alone and not always in healthy ways. But God was here and let me know He would protect me from what and who was hurting me. He would protect me physically and in all areas of my well-being. God would put others in my path to do so as well. He poured into me knowledge and wisdom through books, studies, and, most importantly, His word. I clung to scripture and to His command not to lie on the floor and wallow in my sadness. I was to put on a crown I never knew I had and walk, knowing that I am His princess, His daughter.

At the same time God was teaching me what I meant to Him, my dad here on earth kept reminding me of the scriptures, such as:

"But because of his great love for us, God, who is rich in mercy, made us alive with Christ even when we were dead in transgressions—it is by grace you have been saved. And God raised us up with Christ and seated us with him in the heavenly realms in Christ Jesus."—Ephesians 2: 4-6 (NIV)[9]

This was directly in line with the ideas God was teaching me.

I clung to this scripture as God built me up and allowed me to raise my head a little higher (something I had never done before), knowing no one could get to me without first going through Him. Then, finally, feelings of reluctant peace won over fear. I saw the light at the end of the tunnel, a light that was completely invisible before. Finally, I could say I *knew* God was on my side and would protect me from what was to come. I mentioned earlier I thought I knew all these things in my heart, but came to find out, I had only been going off what I heard others say and hoped were true. Now, they were becoming fact and what I call "soul-seared." He repeatedly proved Himself, and these truths were burned permanently into my memory and soul, never to be forgotten.

Thinking about my daughter, knowing how I felt about her and all I would do to protect her made it easier for me to understand the protection, love, and acceptance God was offering. If I would do anything in the world for her, there is no way He would do any less for me. The Bible even tells us:

"If you, then, though you are evil, know how to give good gifts to your children, how much more will your Father in heaven give good gifts to those who ask him!?"—Matthew 7:11 (NIV)[8]

I grew stronger and stronger in my confidence in Him and myself. Reading scripture now meant I could picture myself deserving of His word. The stories held lessons I could figure out for myself and realize how they could help me in my life. I quit reading the Bible as stories of people long ago who had nothing to do with me and began reading it as stories of brothers, sisters, friends, relatives, and their Father. I could see how their Father taught, loved, and disciplined them. Knowing this helped me understand what I could expect in my life. This knowledge brought confidence that if He would go to all the trouble to call me His child, then it was not such a stretch to believe He would love and protect me as one. I had never experienced decent self-esteem, and for my entire life, I walked with my head down, eyes to the ground, because I didn't dare assume someone would want to make eye contact with me. But, for a little while, I challenged myself to raise my head, lift my eyes, and walk in a way that showed what I believed to be accurate. He loved me. He would protect me. I was His.

Pause and Ponder

- Can you see God has labeled you royalty even if you do not feel or act royal?
- Can you believe it does not matter how you feel or act because, once He determines something, no one else can change it? Or do you still not believe what scripture says about you?
- Can you name what protection you long for right now?

Well, that was not what I expected.

If you had told me it was all a joke and God would eventually tell me He was only saying all the princess stuff just to get me to do what He wanted, I would have believed you. It would have been what I expected and what I was used to. Humans tend to teach us this lesson, do they not? What I did not expect, though, was what happened next. He never once let me down. He never once said it was all a joke or a manipulation. What He did say is something I never could have guessed.

After weeks of being built up and taught who I was, there came a time when I would have to face someone I did not want to face. This person was part of why I was on the floor crying out to God in despair just a few weeks before. More and more had come to light of all the betrayal happening, and while I would not have chosen to face this person again, it was not something I could avoid. So I prayed. I explained to God I simply could not do it. I could not face them. I would lose everything I had gained, and I could not emotionally deal with going backward. Then a sly little smirk came over my face as I sensed God ask me, "Do you remember everything I said about you?

All the things I would do to anyone who tried to mess with you?" I remembered and was happy to know I had nothing to fear, but they did. They would have to deal with the wrath of The King and all the forces under His power if they dared mess with me! I proudly remembered all I had learned about being a princess and the privileges accompanying it. Now, I was ready to face them and anything else headed my way!

Then, God asked, "Do you remember what I said I would do to anyone who tried to mess with you?" I again found myself saying, "Yes, sir." I was excited to know I could feel protected from others for once. This was not a situation where I had to wonder if I was worth it or chosen. He had shown me He would choose me. *I* was important enough, *I* was loved enough, and He was faithful enough to follow through. So, I beamed with pride and waited for what He would say next.

I can't help but wonder where you are right now in your own life. Are you dealing with an equally devastating situation? Are you struggling to see yourself as worthy of protection and love? Or maybe you never even considered the possibility, because protection is a luxury you could not afford. I wish I could sit with you right now and hear what you are facing or have faced in your life. I wish I could sit face to face and share with you and tell you if no one else ever has, I will fight for you and with you. While, unfortunately, I cannot sit with everyone, I can offer you my truth: I refused to admit I was desperate for the level of love God was offering because no one had ever offered it to me before.

I thought that kind of love was only true in fairy tales and movies. I still have this belief, in a sense. The difference is the fairytale is real, but the prince is not who we expected. He is riding in to swoop us up and take us to a place of unconditional love and protection. Can you allow yourself to imagine it? I want to sincerely say to you–it does not

SIMMER IN IT | 41

matter if you are sitting on the street hoping for your next fix, if you are hiding in the bathroom reading this to escape your kids, if you just got out of Sunday service and felt like a fraud, or even if you are sitting in your very own palace with all your physical needs met and exceeded beyond your imagination - desperation and devastation are not looking for a specific type of person as they roam this earth. They are equal opportunity evils that will attack anyone at any time. But Sister, we have hope. Please keep reading and hoping.

Much like myself, you may have to face someone or something you do not feel equipped to face. To the one who has an upcoming court date potentially changing the course of their life forever, to the one who is facing an unexpected career change, to the one who has to face the enemy in the flesh, may you take the time to solidify who you are beforehand. Sit in the truth of being the princess He says you are. Shut the voices down who say He could never love someone like you because you are exactly the one He smiles because of. He knows and sees the you who has been ignored for so long. The you no one else can see. And you make Him smile. The little girl inside with her pretty dress, high-heel shoes, and crown, or her blue jeans, Converse, and crown... no matter how the princess inside you looks, she makes Him smile... and He will defend her at all costs. I will even go so far as to tell you that church, religion, and some of the Christians you have met do not get to define you. Maybe they have been telling you to act like a good Christian girl, and when you fail, they turn their back on you. Sister, that is not God. When you fail, He is waiting for you to come home, to come to Him, to let Him take care of things. He has never said to straighten up or clean up before you come home. He calls you to come home, and He will create in you and present you as the princess you are.

Please read Luke 15:11-32. This is a story Jesus tells as an example of the way God loves us. It is a parable, which is a storytelling style that Jesus used frequently to example a life lesson with the people listening.

Pause and Ponder

- Is it easier to believe it is all a joke than to perceive yourself as someone who has been adopted into the wealthiest, purest, and most glorious kingdom ever?
- Do you find it silly to think of yourself in this way?
- Commit to yourself that you will take some time this week to remind yourself that He calls you His child. Also, remind yourself what it means to be His child. This will be crucial to the next step, so challenge yourself not to skip this part, no matter how much easier it would be. The way to know is to look it up in scripture and ask people you can trust.

What now?

Can I tell you how proud I am of you? You have finished this chapter (I don't care how long it took you). You have worked hard and dug deep to ask yourself some hard questions. Do not dismiss the growth from your efforts. Whether you skimmed through the chapter or dove in and took the time to do the work... you deserve to celebrate YOU and your efforts!

- Take a deep breath and thank God for the work He is doing.

- Praise Him because He loves you, cares for you, protects you, and encourages you.
- Rest in this knowledge. Take some time to simmer in it this week and repeat it to yourself over and over if necessary. Trust me; this is crucial to the next steps.

Prayer

Father, I praise You for the grace and kindness You show even though I do not deserve it. You came in and offered me a place in Your family when I felt unwanted and unworthy of kindness and acceptance. May I take this gift and hold on to it lovingly and respectfully, always remembering You will never take it away, that I will never deserve it, yet I can honor it and You, but not without Your help. I pray You show me how to walk in the knowledge I am wanted at Your family gatherings exactly the way I look and act at this very moment. No cleanup is required.

Amen

The Princess put on the crown she had long since forgotten, reminding her she would forever have royal blood, which gives the right to royal protection, training, and provision. She then set her sights on learning about the heritage she never knew existed and the family welcoming her home. Hope was back, although sheepish at first. Adoption into a royal family might not be so bad. After all, she was created as a joint heir with the King's son Himself! Learning to let go of beliefs that said otherwise was freeing beyond her imagination!

Chapter 3

He Loves YOU Wildly, Fiercely, and Deeply

"And God raised us up with Christ and seated us with him in the heavenly realms in Christ Jesus, in order that in the coming ages he might show the incomparable riches of his grace, expressed in his kindness to us in Christ Jesus."—Ephesians 2:6-7 (NIV)[10]

Expectation. I can almost see the weight of it as a physical entity crawling up my spine to the base of my neck and spreading through my shoulders. Simultaneously, down my arms and across my chest, rolling through my body and mind much like a heavy fog rolls across a lake. Once the feeling reaches a spot in my heart, deep in the middle of my chest, it has reached my last line of defense. Then the actual war begins. I should never allow it to get this far. I pretend that the first line of defense–usually ignoring the situation or stuffing it down by numbing in some way, should stop it–but clearly, it cannot. The second, third, fourth, and fifth lines of defense are also useless. Simmering in my faults and failures, trying to bargain with the enemy, giving up to make space for someone who deserves more success, releasing my frustration through complaining or lashing out–none of these ever work. The enemy, a prowling, growling, spreading creature, seeps into my pores, blood, and thoughts–and reaches out for my soul. It multiplies and spreads its most effective poison, which emits much toxicity even though it weakens in its potency because it recognizes what it has finally come up against. As a last-ditch effort, Expectation whispers into my depths, saying:

- *You are not what you should be.*
- *You know you are not who you thought you would be.*
- *Do you actually believe your God will accept you crawling back again? Didn't you just do this yesterday? This exact thing?*

Friends, I am tired. I am weak. There is a physical hurt deep within that no pain medication or numbing can touch. Once again, whether I deserve it or not, The Holy Spirit, the most powerful asset we have–the one I tend to save as my last line of defense–takes His stand. The Holy Spirit stands up to my enemy, Expectation, blocking it from a spot deep in my chest where my soul is guarded. He can, with simple words, cause Expectation to cringe, to seethe, to retreat, but it never goes quietly. It digs its claws in and rips and tears as it is forced back. It retreats–not quickly, not painlessly, but it retreats.

My hope is the place deep in my chest... the tiny little spot holding my soul, surrounded by The Holy Spirit, will finally be allowed to relocate to the front lines. I need to do some tactical maneuvering. I need to rotate my defenses and allow my last line of defense to become my first.

God and prayer always seem to be my last line of defense. The last place I turn to when I am struggling, because shouldn't I be strong enough to handle this on my own? Shouldn't I be a strong enough Christian and have enough faith not to have to ask Him to save me from every single thing? Won't He be disappointed if I am not strong enough to handle this? I use God and His Spirit as my last line of defense because I was told to do so. Guess who told me I should? Expectation. It told me I should be able to stand up for myself. If I were a good Christian, if I were truly "Christ-like," I could guard myself. Then, as soon as I think I am strong enough to do it alone, as is expected of a strong Christian, I trip and I fall because I tried to stand without Jesus.

Man! This is a great attack strategy! To convince a person to act in a way they know is wrong, then condemn them for falling for it. (Humans do this to us as well, do they not?) Well, now it's acknowledged! An attacker's best weapon is surprise, but now I'm calling this one out and refusing to be surprised by it any longer! Scripture says:

"Be alert and of sober mind. Your enemy the devil prowls around like a roaring lion looking for someone to devour."—1 Peter 5:8 (NIV)[11]

How often does Expectation creep into your life? Either the expectations you put on yourself or the ones others have said you have to live up to?

My prayers are for God to become my first line of defense. I am asking Him to forgive me because I allowed myself to have such a warped sense of thinking, and I thought I could fight alone. I am asking for the wisdom to realize when I am falling into this trap again because, how many times must I fall for the same thing? Expectation dug a hole for me to fall in, and I did repeatedly. Now it's time for a bob-and-weave maneuver to allow Expectation to fall into its own trap.

Getting Rid of Expectations

Maybe it goes back to being a "good Christian girl." We are so often told how we should act—yet are rarely taught the difference between acting and being.

For now, we must focus on releasing those expectations and wrong beliefs we have lived with for so long. These beliefs will keep us farther from God instead of being closer to Him. This will take some time. Allow yourself grace to sit and pray and think over all of those beliefs. And decide what is true and what is not. We cannot undo a lifetime of wrong beliefs in one sitting, but we can hit the high points, which can be significant steps in the right direction.

I'll start. I used to believe:

- Acting like the people in authority told me to would make me acceptable to God .
- People who went to church and held positions within the church were the authority on right and wrong.
- God wanted me to sit down and be quiet since the people in my life wanted me to.
- I became likable by choosing not to defend myself when someone treated me poorly.
- Loving and accepting someone, no matter how they treated me, was what God would want me to do.
- When I messed up, God would turn His back on me.
- Because I did not have a position of title, my voice didn't matter, and I could never know as much as those with positions of authority. No matter how much I studied, somehow, they would always know more.

- Being a good Christian meant I needed to look, act, and think in line with the way others decided I should .

Honestly, I could go on, and on, AND ON about the beliefs I had and the standards I held myself to—which were unattainable. There is no way I could have been the perfect version of the human I believed others were expecting of me (and I was expecting of myself). It was impossible.

Realizing I could not meet these expectations—and I never would—was humbling and challenging for me. What was the purpose, then? What was I supposed to be working for? What made me worthy of love if I could never attain these goals? Did this mean I was hopeless?

Nothing

The reality was, nothing I did could make me a "good Christian girl." Nothing I accomplished or worked for would ever get me the approval I sought. Of course, if I acted in the way the people around me wanted me to, then I might gain their approval—for a bit. The problem is their idea of how I should act could change from one day to the next. It most certainly changed from one person to the next. When I had it all figured out with one person in my life, another person came along, and they believed entirely differently. I was not acting as they thought I should, and now it felt as if I was back to disappointing someone. It felt as if it was always something, changing from day to day—and sometimes it was me.

Finally, as God took me through learning who I was, these expectations slowly but surely revealed themselves and fell away. I've learned the people here on this earth with me are only humans, and yes, they make mistakes, and yes, they are sometimes wrong, and yes, they put unrealistic expectations on other people and themselves. But you know what? I have a choice if I get sucked into it or not. I did not always believe there was a choice. I am thankful God showed me all these humans around me are as flawed as I am. They are not Him, and they do not hold the ultimate authority on who I should be, how I should act, or what makes me a good or bad person.

It was a relief to realize I did not have to be thrown about by every whim and new belief someone else had. I thrived on the fact there was a way to know who I should be and how I should act, and it never changed. I never had to guess about it. I never had to conform, depending on who I was around, and did not have to wonder what I should believe. Once I realized that everything I needed to know about myself, I could find out for myself in scripture–it brought unexpected peace. I no longer had to have the spirit of expectation crawling up my spine and whispering in my ear. I could be free and have peace, knowing it was not as hard as I had been making it out to be.

As an example, I remember in an elementary-age Sunday School one day, the lesson taught was about "backsliders" (if you have never heard the term, it often refers to a believer not faithfully attending church and/or not living their life as others think they should be living) and how it is a sin to not go to church, or at least this is how my child brain translated the teaching. The term "backslider" has stuck with me my entire life. After the lesson, we colored a picture of a man packing his boat up to go to the lake instead of going to church. I did not know this was a metaphor, and before I knew it, I had a longstanding belief that fishing on a Sunday was a sin. She was teaching small children, and using an example we could connect with. I am the one who took it out of context and created a long-held belief because of it. There is nowhere in scripture saying that fishing on a Sunday is a sin. Scripture tells us about having a Sabbath day for rest and honoring God. It also tells us to remember to gather with fellow believers. But in my mind, going fishing on a Sunday was a sin. Period. It didn't matter that some people consider the Sabbath to be on Saturday, gatherings with fellow believers can be done on a different day, or not all churches gather in the same way. This may seem like a silly example, but it shows how easily we develop a belief in our minds based on very little evidence.

Another aspect of this story is my understanding of 'sin.' There I was, thinking this man was in so much trouble with God because he sinned. No one taught me that 'sin' means 'to miss the mark.' We tend to hear it and think it means God is mad at us. But in reality, it is a sporting term used when someone shoots an arrow, and it does not hit the bullseye. That's it. It means God knows what is best for us, and when we do not listen, we are missing the mark on what is best–He is not mad at us. Of course, He wants us to make a bullseye because it means we will be closer to living a life of wisdom, love, and grace. Which means we will be closer to Him. Should we try to hit the bullseye? Yes. Is He mad at us when we don't? No. Is He happy to teach us pointers and strategies to become better? One hundred percent yes. Again, He wants what is best for us because of His love, not so He can condemn us.

There are instances in scripture where God has to turn away because people choose the blatant desire to sin. These instances are different from trying to do right but failing. It takes practice to get a consistent action down–like when trying to hit the bullseye of a target. He will help guide us and teach us as we practice. This is not the same as throwing your bow and arrow down, mocking the fact that He wanted to equip you with the skills needed to survive in this world and refusing to try again.

Was my Sunday School teacher wrong for what she taught? No, she was doing her best to teach at our level. My clinging to the belief and putting unrealistic expectations on myself was not her fault. She was not intentionally trying to manipulate. If she knew we had established an unrealistic belief and allowed it to continue, then she would have been wrong. One of the most common phrases Mom asked me growing up was, "Where do you come up with this stuff?" so I know I tend to have a bit of imagination. This was not the teacher's fault.

An example of someone intentionally trying to manipulate you would be a spouse who considers themselves the spiritual authority in the home, and they use scripture to belittle you and make you feel inferior. Or maybe they don't believe in the Bible but will say things like, "Your Bible says you should...but you never do it! Your God can never love or accept you!" These are examples of a type of spiritual abuse and not at all the way Jesus handled people He encountered. As with any kind of abuse, always find a trusted Christian counselor to help maneuver these relationships.

Do you remember the visit I was preparing for in the last chapter and I left you by saying what came next differed from what I expected–see there is that word again–*Expectation.* Always trying to manipulate, lie, and create division. I had been learning so much about who I was and the lengths God would go to for my protection, so what He told me as I prepared for the visit I was dreading so much blindsided me.

The Holy Spirit whispered this one profound statement to me. He asked me, "Do you remember everything I taught you about being My child? Do you remember the lengths I said I would go for your protection?" As I felt pretty special and proudly said 'yes, Sir,' I heard Him say, "I would do the same for them. Don't make me have to protect them from you."

Woah! This was not exactly what I expected to hear, and it was certainly different from what I *wanted* to hear! Yet, hearing those words did not bring the feelings of rejection they usually would have brought. Before all I had recently learned, I would have immediately assumed it had all been a lie, and He was telling me He loved this other person more than me. God had done too much work for me to return to that place, though. Instead of regret and fear, what swept over me was peace, confidence, and knowing. I knew all He had been teaching was still true. I was still loved and protected beyond my comprehension–but so were they. He loved them equally. I didn't like it, but I respected it.

Interestingly, this lesson brought peace because knowing He loved them equally meant He was not like others who changed their minds daily. He was not someone who had different rules for different people. No, if He says He loves you, He loves you. Wildy, fiercely, and deeply.

Please notice I said YOU. He loves YOU wildly, fiercely, and deeply.

Without hesitation, without reservation. Knowing you are not and will likely never meet the expectations of others. And He is glad about that! He doesn't want you to reach their goals for you or to act the way they tell you to. He wants you to know you can't because those expectations are moving targets! *His love for you is not.* There is no guessing; there is knowing. The same applies to them also, though. All the resentment you have been harboring because they should have known better or done better and all the hurt you have and your expectations for them do not change His love for them, just like it doesn't change His love for you. Does this mean sin doesn't exist, and we should allow others to treat us however they want? Nope. What it does mean, though, is we can release ourselves and them from all those expectations, set the healthy boundaries we need, and allow Him to do the work of restoring anything needing to be restored.

I do not know about you, but I never want to be the person He has to defend another from because I know the lengths He will go to for the protection of His children.

(I doubt I need to clarify this, but in case I do, I am not condoning abuse or anything that breaks the law. You should immediately remove yourself from any abusive situation.)

Pause and Ponder

- What wrong beliefs or wrong expectations do you need to forgive yourself for?
- What expectations do you need to let go of?
- What unattainable or non-biblical expectations have others had for you that you need to let go of?
- Any expectations you move forward with (and yes, we should have healthy and moral beliefs and expectations for ourselves) should be able to be backed up by scripture. Read to see what scripture says about how we should act. Use your favorite method to daily remind yourself of these truths.

Prayer

Thank you, Father, for helping me understand who I am to You and who those around me are as well. I ask Your forgiveness for the times I put my happiness above the needs of others. I also ask Your forgiveness for the times I have neglected or abused myself to the extent I was in no shape to have anything to offer You. I know You have asked for nothing in return for the gift You gave me, but I am so grateful, and I want to be a better example and show You how much I appreciate You giving me another chance. Father, I need to forgive myself and others for the incorrect beliefs I have held. I need to understand what they are, let go of them, and replace them with Your truth. As I read Your Word, I ask for wisdom to understand when I feel overwhelmed or confused. Thank You that I know Your word says I can trust You to give wisdom because it says,

"For the LORD gives wisdom; from his mouth come knowledge and understanding."—Proverbs 2:6 (NIV)[12]

The polished crown can be worn a bit more confidently now that she realizes the King loves her and can speak truth into her life. Real truth. Unchained truth. The princess spent every moment she could at His side, having craved this REAL love and affection for so very long. The princess discovered Prince Charming in God and she planned never to leave His side. Together, they set their sights on a royal hunt where instead of hunting for those who should be purged from The Kingdom; she determined to, with Him, hunt for all the lost crowns and return them to their rightful owners, thus allowing all to know they were equal in this Kingdom where everyone sits together in Heavenly places.

Section 1

Scripture Reading

Learn About Your Heritage... Yes, Yours

Suggested Reading: Genesis 37

You will hear me say that taking one scripture from a random place in the Bible and deciding to use it alone is not the way to read scripture. We should set our sights on all the Bible offers us. It is so rich and exciting once you get familiar with it; the more familiar you get, the more you want to continue. When beginning with the first book, we get to delve in and get to know each character just as if we were binge-watching the latest series. From time to time, though, I will use individual scriptures because when I had nothing else to cling to, I could cling to those scriptures similar to the ones I share throughout this book. I felt they were all I had; those individual scriptures built my desire for more. So I say this: when a single scripture is all you can manage, then, girl, you cling to that scripture and hold on with all you've got. But don't let it be where you stay. Keep building, and read the scriptures in front of it and behind it when you can. Read the entire chapter and see how it was used in the lives of those in the Bible. We seem surprised sometimes when the one scripture we are clinging to was intended for another person at another time. It is so cool to read about those people and the similarities between their lives and ours.

For example, did you know Joseph (one of the many rulers in the Bible) was not born into royalty? His siblings hated that he had dreams about ruling over them. How could he rule over them if he was younger and not born as royalty? Sound familiar? People around us will argue there is no way we deserve the royal treatment. They will wonder who exactly we think we are, which is okay. Their treatment of us does not make us royal or strip royalty from us. We can't expect them to treat us in a way they don't understand. This land is not where we rule. We are royals in a spiritual realm. The more we learn who we are, the more we can share with them who they are as well.

In Section One's suggested scripture reading, we will read about Joseph and his relationship with his brothers. If you continue to read the following few chapters of the Bible's story of Joseph, you will see how God turned his situation around. This is such a relatable story of God's protection and grace. If you don't read the full story, know this: when others do not see it, or we cannot see it ourselves, we do deserve the royal protection God offers (not because we are who others say we should be, but because we are His). Eventually, its purposes reveal themselves, and we can use it for His glory and the benefit of others.

TIP:

View the Bible as a journal. A journal God has kept throughout the generations, where He shares about His children, all the things He has created, the loss of His son, etc. Much like the same type of thoughts we share in our own journals. He discusses how difficult His kids can be and how much He longs for them to do what is right and come home. He talks about how to handle situations where you feel alone and desperate. How to handle loss, failure, and so much more. Once I began viewing scripture this way, it helped me understand why it is so important to read. This process also made it easier to comprehend and connect with. It's okay if it does not come easy at first. Keep going. Keep connecting. You will be amazed at how much will become clear as you do.

Section 2:

The Battlefield

Chapter 4

The Battle

"For our struggle is not against flesh and blood, but against the rulers, against the authorities, against the powers of this dark world and against the spiritual forces of evil in the heavenly realms,"
—Ephesians 6:12 (NIV)[13]

A raging battlefield on a rolling hillside. The scenery is gorgeous, with green grassy hills covered in those delicate, little purple and white flowers that sprout up wildly in their own perfect time each year. Juxtaposed is the battle itself. It is bloody. Bodies lie scattered about, contorted in unnatural ways – bloody and badly wounded. There is no medic there to help. They simply lie there struggling to breathe, dying. Soldiers are on each side, fiercely battling with swords, knives, guns, and even their hands. When I pictured this scene, immediately what came to my mind was an old history book from school where there were illustrations of battlefields from the Civil War. This was not sophisticated, modern warfare with high-tech weapons and biological agents. This was grotesque, hand-to-hand combat, with mass casualties from both sides. One man stands on a hill, far across the battlefield. I look at what is happening around me–wondering why he stands there watching–appearing to help in no way.

I somehow know my only mission is to get to him. I know if I do, I will find peace and protection. Like when you were a young child, running to home base while playing tag–I know that no harm can come there. I can breathe, regain my strength, and cheer on my friends with no fear of 'It' getting me. No matter what, no matter how–I must get to him. I resolve deep in my soul to fight with all I have to get to the other side of this battlefield. To the man I have a deep knowing must be Jesus.

I began fighting and clawing my way toward Jesus. Fighting through demons, minions, and all things evil who are trying to keep me from getting to Him. I fought with all I have, swinging my sword, taking blows, standing back up, and moving forward until I finally, breathless and wounded, reached Him. I was grateful to get there and extremely exhausted. Pulling myself up by clinging onto Him, I fully expected to hear those words we are told we will hear when we stand before God. "Well done, my good and faithful servant." To my horror, I didn't hear those words. What I heard cut me to the core. Jesus looks at me and asks, "Where have you been?"

Where have I been?! Did He just ask me that? I was devastated! Without even looking, I flung my arm in the direction of the bloody battlefield I had come from and exclaimed, "I've been fighting my way to You! All those demons, all those circumstances, all those hurts trying to beat me down and keep me from You; THAT is where I have been!" With a gentle yet confused tone, He asks, "What demons? What circumstances?" Exasperated, I point to the battlefield and exclaim, "THOSE DEMONS!"

As I turn my head and the words leave my mouth, I finally look and realize there is nothing there. The battlefield is empty. No battle. No bodies. No blood. Just a peaceful and beautiful rolling countryside. Confused and even more exasperated, I ask, "What happened? I JUST fought my way here! I JUST fought all the demons and battles! I'm exhausted! I was badly wounded, but I made it here to YOU!"

He gently states, "I already fought and won those battles for you. All you had to do was walk to Me. You chose to fight because you felt you had to. You wanted to feel you were doing it alone and earning your way here. In reality, they could not touch you. You simply had to walk to Me."

Pause and Ponder

I don't know if another lesson has been as useful to me as this one. No matter what the circumstance, this lesson rings true every time.

- What unwinnable battle are you fighting currently? Are you exhausted and worn down from the constant fight?
- Does it appear there is no other option than for you to be the one to pick up the sword and fight for those around you? Maybe your marriage, your children, yourself?

We all have a raging battle around us—sometimes it is even within us. Some of us are in seemingly hopeless, dire situations. And I will not diminish your struggle. What I will say, friend, is to trust Him in the fight! But remember, above all, the battle is already won. He sees your every tear; you are not forgotten. He goes before you, fighting on your behalf every step of the way. These may sound like nice little church quotes people often spew, but my experience tells me otherwise. These words were and are life-giving truths.

Prove It

Unfortunately, there appears to be a puzzling contrast between two particular concepts in the Bible, and they are both shoved down our throats regularly in certain circles. Yet it's challenging to find someone who can explain. I don't promise to do it well, but I will try my best to explain them in the way I understand them to be. This will also help explain why the battle is so important, even when unnecessary.

We can break down the two presented concepts as:
1. I do not have to earn God's love.
2. There are rules I must follow to earn God's love.

Each of these concepts holds truth but seems contradictory to each other, as if they should not, or even could not, simultaneously exist. The question tends to be, which is it? Do I have to prove myself to Him or not? While there is no simple yes or no answer to this question, let's try to break it down.

Concept 1: I do not have to earn God's love.

Scripture tells us, *"You see, at just the right time, when we were still powerless, Christ died for the ungodly. Rarely will anyone die for a righteous person, though for a good person someone might possibly dare to die. But God demonstrates his own love for us in this: While we were still sinners, Christ died for us."*—Romans 5:6-8 (NIV)[14]

70 | FEARLESSLY BECOMING

These scriptures are a beautiful example of the concept that you do not have to earn God's love. *"While we were still sinners, Christ died for us."* If you go out Saturday night, get drunk, and have a one-night stand, would you feel comfortable with instead of doing the walk of shame back home, you walk straight into church instead? Same party clothes, same breath smelling of alcohol, same smeared lipstick. Society might say "NO WAY." God says while you are still a sinner, Christ died for you! You are not required to clean up, quit a habit, put your best clothes on, clean up your language, lose weight, or try to look or act the part in any other way. You are welcome as you are–to realize you need Him and to approach Him. He is your father, the King, yes, but He is Love! He welcomes you in love with open arms! This proves to us we do NOT have to earn God's love!

Scripture has taught me, and He has shown me over and over, that He loves me no matter what. Through my poor attitudes and poor decisions He loves me just as I am. Broken, joyful, sad, overwhelmed. He loves lavishly and extravagantly through it all.

Concept 2: There are rules I must follow to earn God's love.

Most of us have heard of the 10 Commandments, which are found in Exodus 20. These are 10 rules that use words like "you shall not," which lets us know these rules are not up for debate. You can also read in Ephesians where it says things such as *"Do not let unwholesome talk come out of your mouths, but only what is helpful for building others up according to their needs, that it may benefit those who listen."* (Ephesians 4:29 NIV). Has unwholesome (destructive, improper) talk ever come out of your mouth? We can look down a few lines in scripture and see in verse 31 where it says, "Get rid of all bitterness, rage, and anger, brawling and slander, along with every form of malice." Have you ever

THE BATTLE | 71

argued with someone? Have you ever been angry with them? I don't know about you, but I could raise my hand about each action listed in the scriptures above. If you, too, are guilty of each of these, please know that God still loves you because He is God and you do not have to prove one thing to Him.

As a child of God, however, there are commandments (rules/ways of living) that we must follow to stay on His path. Will He love us if we stray? Absolutely. As humans, God understands our sinful and fragile nature and longs to draw us near through repentance and turning back to Him.

Do you want to know what will happen? *Because He loves you no matter what,* you will begin seeing that you want to change. You might notice that your heart softens toward people you previously hated. You might notice that old habits no longer have the hold on you they once did. Maybe that cigarette that previously hit the spot now has a horrible flavor to you. Maybe those friends that you always partied with suddenly move away or take a job that doesn't fit your schedule anymore. While you are not changing in order to earn His love, He is helping you improve your life because He loves you. Sister, every story I have shared in this book has happened during my life as a Christian. But through all of it, I have found peace and have learned to go to Him for help more and more. All the "you shall not" rules in scripture do not keep Him from loving me. They keep me from self-destructing and they keep me from disrespecting His love for me. If I do not follow them, He still loves me. But am I being loving toward Him?

He has rescued me physically and removed me from a situation or health crisis. Sometimes, He rescued me emotionally and mentally by strengthening my mind to handle what I was dealing with. Sometimes, He rescued me spiritually, not by removing me from the situation or removing the pain, but by standing right there with me, reminding me of what His word says and allowing me to grow strong in it. No matter what you get yourself into and no matter what happens–He loves you wildly, fiercely, and deeply. You, in turn, will find more and more ways to express your love for Him as well.

Pause and Ponder

- I hope my explanation is helpful. If so, do you agree with it or see God's love differently than I do?
- Have you been told you don't have to earn His love–but then also told that if you don't act a certain way, look a certain way, or worship a certain way, you are wrong? Or worse, He could never love you?
- Is there a time in your life you can look back on and realize even though it seems horrible, you learned a valuable lesson or grew?
- Can you see the difference between having to earn His love and asking for His help?
- If you have attempted to earn His love by an action of some sort, would you be willing to take a minute to forgive yourself? Or forgive someone who made you believe you had to?
- Are you at a place where you need to turn to Him and ask for help, understanding He knows what will ultimately be the best way?

We must regularly forgive ourselves for forgetting we do not have to look or act a certain way for Him to love us. He loves you; He loves us... period. Yet, we are so honored that we want to show Him respect, gratitude, and worship. Offering respect, gratitude, and worship

THE BATTLE | 73

broadens and strengthens our relationship and how we interact with Him.

Moving On

After I gained a better understanding of God's love for me, that He doesn't force me to be a certain way or work for His love, it became apparent to me it was time I commit myself to God on a different level than I had before.

He showed me how much He loved, protected, and fought for me, and I wanted to know what I could offer to Him. I began seeing I could offer time, attention, and commitment. My (now ex) husband and I were separated during this time, so I was at a place in life where I could spend more time reading the Bible, searching out friends who would draw me closer to God, not away from Him, giving back to other people, and more. Not because any of this was required for Him to love me, but it was required, just as in any relationship, if I wanted to get to know Him better and understand more about Him. I learned to plan what I called God dates. When my daughter was with her father or my parents, I would set aside time for a meal, or a drive, or anything where I could have an empty seat close to me to invite Him to sit with me, and I would talk to God. I would tell Him all that was going on, what I was worried about and hoped for. I don't mean I bowed my head and prayed. No, I talked to Him as if He were sitting there next to me–right there with me. Sometimes, I would listen to music I could sing to Him. Sometimes, I laid my head on an empty chair as if on His knee and cried my immense sorrow out to Him. And sometimes, I sat silently and simply listened with my soul. I grew closer to God during this time than ever before and possibly even since. I still look back on that time with so much fondness, even though it was one of the absolute hardest times I have ever lived through.

Pause and Ponder

- Do you have the time to spend with Him, as mentioned? Even if for a few moments on your drive to work or while you shower?
- What things do you want to pour your soul out to Him about right now?
- Can you see He loves you exactly how you are?
- If not, I want to assure you I have yet to find a place where Jesus asked anyone in scripture to look a certain way before coming to Him. He truly, 100% loves you exactly as you are.

Prayer

Father God, thank You. Thank You for Your protection, Your mercy, and Your unyielding power to demolish all obstacles in the way of Your plan! Never do I want to be against You. I pray You help me see the areas I need to get my eyes on You and make my way to You, knowing You will make a way where there seems to be no way.

The Princess learns the battlefield can look and feel unimaginably fearful, yet when remembering 'eyes on Him,' there is nothing too big to get through. She has learned The King does not require her to work to gain His approval but how beautiful those moments are when they, hand in hand, work to serve others in the kingdom. Feeding a hungry friend, loving on a neighbor, or studying together. The work feels like joy, and the relationship grows deep.

Chapter 5

Battle Scars

"Finally, brothers and sisters, whatever is true, whatever is noble, whatever is right, whatever is pure, whatever is lovely, whatever is admirable—if anything is excellent or praiseworthy—think about such things."
—Phillippians 4:8 (NIV)[15]

I was bloody and bruised from the battle I had encountered. I was exhausted, overwhelmed, and still reeling from all I had seen and learned. As I looked at myself and all the wounds, both seen and unseen, a question slowly rose to the top of my mind.

How many of those wounds were self-inflicted?

What a bizarre thought. None of them were. I saw the battlefield and the enemy who occupied it. I lived the lessons and the struggles that left marks. Then, the term 'friendly fire' came to mind. Again, weird. I decided to simmer in those thoughts for a moment and pray for Him to show me what they might mean in this instance. I began remembering the times I would say things to myself, like,

"If you were a better Christian, this would have never happened to you,"

"If you had prayed more,"

"If you had gone to church more,"

"You are still dealing with addictions which are sinful, and He won't help you until you quit."

"Have you looked at yourself lately? No one would ever believe you were a Christian with the way you look."

"You didn't read your Bible this morning; there is no point in even praying. He won't listen."

Friendly fire. These wounds were not coming from an outside enemy, but from me. I was the one beating myself up from the inside out. With all that was happening outside of me, WHY would I sit and wound myself also?

Do you want to know why?

Partly because it is what I was taught to do. I watched other Christians, all their lives, sacrifice themselves in the name of being "enough" for God. *You are enough.* He deserves perfection, but He loves us as we are. I listened to lesson after lesson about expectations for Christians, about how all the men and women of the Bible fought the good fight and honored God. Often left out of the story was the daily, torturous fight they had to go through to earn their spot in Scripture.

I learned David fought Goliath and, with God's help, won. What I did not learn until much later was the mental and emotional struggles David had for much of his life. His best friend's dad hated him, and he was forced to move and live in hiding. He joined up with the very people he had hated previously. Even after he was king, he had an affair with another man's wife and killed the husband in a diabolical way, hoping to get away with the affair. What else does the Bible say about David? He was a man after God's own heart. In 1 Samuel 13:14, God is speaking with Saul and letting him know David will replace him as king because David is a man after God's own heart.

When reading about David, it does not take long to see how many ways David messed up in his life. With all the sins he committed, how is it possible for him to be considered a man after God's heart? Because each time he messed up, David recognized his sin (missing the mark) and turned back to God. Now, did he know having an affair was wrong? Yes. Did he have time to stop himself before he followed through? Yes. I wonder how often we have been caught up in the moment and made a poor decision? One we knew was wrong, but did anyway? Then, it is as if the fog clears from our mind, and we think, *"What did I do?!"* At the moment a decision arises, we can stop and choose to do what we know is right–or not. If we end up making the wrong decision, we then can decide what to do next. Turn to God or hide from Him. I have not found a single time in Scripture where hiding from God worked out well. Yet, turning to God brings examples of redemption time and time again.

Pause and Ponder

The above exemplifies friendly fire as negative self-talk. It is a skill I have honed very well throughout life and one I definitely could have done without! What about you?

- Do you recognize negative self-talk in yourself?
- Is this something shown to you by others, or did you develop it on your own?
- Can you see it is actually you doing the enemy's work for him?

Believe me, I understand how easy it is to get caught up in negative self-talk and how difficult it is to step out of. When I began picturing it as part of the battle–and I was willingly participating with the other team against myself–it helped me focus on a different path. I began seeing my words as arrows either hurting the enemy (words of affirmation, words of love, scriptures, etc.) or helping the enemy (words of self-degradation, hurtful words to others, lies, using scripture out of context and against God).

But Wait, There's More!

Once I could recognize the words I was using and how powerful they were in the battle we were in, there was a bit of a fog-clearing and giving way to more realizations.

Realizations such as:

- My addictions are also considered self-harm. This is when I participate in helping the enemy destroy me.
- Being complacent about environmental inputs is another weapon used against me. (An environmental input is anything outside of yourself that may affect you, your emotions, and your thoughts) This is not something any of us can define for another, but for me, environmental inputs came as unfair expectations from others, being aware of whose teaching I read and listened to, and being intentional about filling my mind and spirit with more truth and love. One change I made early on was the music I listened to. Trust me, I will not be someone who condemns you for the music you listen to. To this day, I still have a very wide range of styles gracing my playlists. However, at one time during my early learning process, God showed

82 | FEARLESSLY BECOMING

me that the secular music I was listening to was doing an excellent job of helping me know I was not alone, others shared my struggles, and I had reason to be frustrated, sad, and angry. Then He added that while all of that may be true and understandable, the secular music I was listening to exemplified where I was. While the music glorifying and honoring Him showed me where I was headed! Woah! Insert dramatic pause. When listening to worship and scripture-filled music, I saw the life I could have with Him instead of wallowing in the life I had been living.

- When all is said and done and I stand before God, I feel confident He will not accept the words, "because someone hurt my feelings," "everyone has always done it that way," or "because it is what I was taught" as an excuse for ignoring what I knew to do. I quickly realized it is my job to study and learn what scripture says instead of simply believing what others teach. I also realized someone else being rude, abusive, or manipulative did not give me a free pass on doing what was right. I can't say, "She would have been mad at me if I told her no," or "If they had treated me better and taught me better as a kid, I would not have done all those wrong things." Others will be held accountable for the choices they make. But I am held accountable, whether on this earth or after, for my choices. I do not get to use someone else as an excuse for not doing what scripture states. Hard truth. But truth nonetheless.

In Chapter 4, we discussed how our actions do not determine if God loves us or not, but our closeness with Him creates in us a hope to honor Him to the best of our ability. That is exactly what we are talking about here as well. As with any relationship, the closer you grow together with God, the more you get to know Him.

Have you ever heard of the "5 Love Languages" book by Gary Chapman? It is a book that many coaches, counselors, and teachers use to teach couples to understand how to show love to one another. The concept teaches we do not all feel loved in the same ways. Some of us like to hold hands or hug–while others may quickly recoil at the mere thought. There are several suggested love languages, and typically two people in a relationship have different ways of giving and receiving love. I like to say that obedience is God's love language. It is a way to show Him and others that we are close enough to Him to have read His word and prayed about or discussed our questions with God or a trusted mentor. We also can show Him love by studying and obeying to the best of our ability. When we are obedient, we come to understand and know His love through His words and the protection they bring.

Pause and Ponder

- Do you recognize ways, other than negative self-talk, you are participating in harming yourself?
- Are there aspects of your life where you realize you should make changes regarding who and what you allow to have input into your life?
- Do you ever believe if others would do what is right, then you would be able to as well? Or blame others for what you do, or do not do, when it comes to right and wrong?
- Are you able to distinguish between the fact that God loves us without demands *and* closeness with Him creates in us a desire to honor Him with our behaviors?

I want to promise you I am keenly aware of the enormity of these statements, and most of us will take days, weeks, months, years, and decades to overcome some of these issues. And friend, that is okay. Recognizing, acknowledging, and asking for forgiveness gets the ball rolling. It is by no means the end, but they are huge beginning steps catapulting you much further down the path with Him.

But Wait, There's More!

Yes—I'm aware I've already made this statement, but it is just as true now as it was a few paragraphs ago. The 'more' is this: I'm not finished with my journey. I have not learned all I need to learn and have not allowed Him to conquer everything I need to let go of. I'm stubborn, set in my ways, and apparently, according to a recent prayer time... I also have a comfort addiction. Ugh. Insert dramatic pause *again*. I could have done without that little revelation, but it is true.

I have an unrealistic expectation that life should be comfortable. Often convinced that things of God should not be difficult. I remember growing up believing God takes away our difficulties, and you can tell someone is walking with God when they have a life of ease. Y'all, this is not true. Truth is, scripture tells us we can identify Christ in someone's life by their fruit (see Galatians 5:23 below). Somewhere along the way, we decided this meant their life looked like a single marriage, and a two-parent home with a house full of perfectly behaved children where no one had any addictions or disorders. They all love each other, their jobs, their church, and they have an amazing group of friends and family surrounding them.

"But the fruit of the Spirit is love, joy, peace, forbearance, kindness, goodness, faithfulness, gentleness and self-control. Against such things there is no law."—Galatians 5:23 (NIV)[16]

This scripture might cause you to picture that perfect person with the perfect family. I would encourage you to read the entire chapter of Galatians 5. Whew! In it, Paul is addressing what is going on in a community called Galatia where He is staying for a while because he became sick on his trip while spreading the gospel. He ended up building churches there and teaching people about the gospel. Many of the people in Galatia had been religious all their lives, so he is talking to those 'good church people' we typically think have it all together. But they did not.

Paul's teaching on this day was about what the church was doing well and where they were failing. You see, they were knowledgeable in the religious laws and customs and were performing as such (which made them feel superior). But this did not mean they were behaving biblically, based on the teachings of Christ. Paul took the time to introduce the city of Galatia to the truth about Jesus and the forgiveness offered through Him.

You see, most of us do not turn our lives around instantly; we try, fail, and try again. How we handle these times tells much more about our spiritual lives than what we are going through. The church in Galatia was the same. They had the head knowledge of the laws, the customs, and the expectations. Yet, they were missing the grace that Christ brought. They were missing the Holy Spirit, who is with us even today, to help guide us. Even they needed time to get their mind, body, and soul on the same page, so to speak. We do too, and that is ok.

Pause and Ponder

- Do you believe you must stop doing what you are doing before God will love and accept you?

- Consider this: you walk into church and see a well-known local business executive who contributes positively to the community and tells nonbelievers about God, yet you know they are having an ongoing affair. You also see a known addict, who is honestly probably high at this very moment, sitting in the same church. Which one deserves to be there? Can I challenge your thinking? Some of us would say the business executive because most of what his life consists of seems positive. Others would say the addict because even though they messed up, they are trying to turn themselves around. Some of us would say neither because they need to address their issues and get right with God. Some of us would say both deserve to be there because the church is where we want anyone who needs to hear the good news about God and who needs and longs to do better. I am of the belief that if I am focused on either one of them I have missed the point entirely. I need to be face down in the dirt at the feet of Jesus because of my own hang ups which are potentially worse than anything they have done. I have been the person who acts like a devout Christian but knows I am doing things I should not, even though most people would never have a clue. Let's invite them in, point them to scripture, and meet them at the feet of Jesus.

- When people say the church is full of hypocrites, my response is "Absolutely it is, because it is full of flawed and broken people." But I don't go to church for the people, and they don't go to church for me. We all meet at a common place to offer our worship and learn about our King Jesus, similar to how sick people meet at a common place to receive treatment for their illnesses. They are not there to fix each other or shame each other into wellness, but because they all need to sit at the feet of the one who heals.

- Can you see the enemy and the friendly fire in these situations– the expectations we put on ourselves and others? The expectations others have put on us that make us believe we are unworthy and unloved.
- Can you challenge yourself to find grace for others? Even for those who do not have grace for you.
- Can you challenge yourself to receive grace when others do not deem you worthy, while challenging yourself to work toward healing, forgiveness, and Him?

Prayer

Jehovah Jireh (the Lord will provide), You deserve all the worship and praise for who You are! I will focus my mind and heart on You to remember that as You provide all I need. I will share Your overflowing goodness with all those around me. I will stop speaking ill of Your children, including myself. I commit to lifting us up to You so You can point out anything needing to be changed and help us to not listen to the negativity from within or without!

In Your mighty name I pray! Amen

After spending her life attempting to duck and dodge all that was coming her way, the Princess was finally shown that many of the attacks on her mind, heart, and soul were coming from the inside. She was firing shot after shot at herself, weakening confidence in herself and God. All the enemy had to do was sit back and laugh as he watched her self-destruct. But no more. Now, she is determined not to make it easy for the enemy to take her down. No longer will she do his work for him. She will remind herself that she respects the King of Kings too much to speak ill of one of His children... even if that child is her.

Chapter 6

On the Other Side of the Battle Field

"You, dear children, are from God and have overcome them, because the one who is in you is greater than the one who is in the world."
—1 John 4:4 (NIV)[17]

The vision I discussed in the last two chapters left out one thing: what the end of the battle looked like and what happened after I walked to Jesus.

What happened next? Honestly, I'm still left hanging in this situation because I find myself in that battle so frequently. I have yet to learn the lessons and put them to practice successfully in all situations. Until I do, I will not see what the other side of the battlefield looks like. It is similar to the movie Groundhog Day, where the same day plays repeatedly until Phil learns to be kind, care for others more than himself, and admits his love to Rita.[18]

Is that what I am destined to do?

Will I be stuck reliving the same mistakes and fighting this battle repeatedly until I get these lessons through my head?

- Eyes on Him
- Don't look around
- We do not war against flesh and blood
- The battle is His
- Eyes on Him (yes, again)
- Keep walking

Pause and Ponder

- Do you feel you keep repeating the same cycles and the same mistakes?
- Are you beaten down by the war that continues to rage?
- How do you survive? Where do you turn for help to make it through?
- Does it help? Or is it part of the lesson you have yet to learn?

Cheeseburgers Do Not Win Battles

It is hard to believe that sometimes our coping mechanisms–those very things we turn to in order to help us feel better or get more emotionally regulated–can be part of the lesson we are supposed to learn instead of the help we need. When we are not careful, these coping mechanisms or vices can become what we worship.

92 | FEARLESSLY BECOMING

My definition of worship is this:

Anything we focus on more than God.

When you are angry, do you suddenly crave a cheeseburger? (I'm raising my hand here) When you are sad, do you have a best friend or occasional buddy you turn to? When someone hurts you, work is especially hard, or the people around you seem to have lost their minds, or there is a health crisis, or a loss—anything at all. Who or what do you turn to? Is prayer your first reaction? Do you reach for your Bible first? Of course, we are to seek wise counsel and have friends. The question is, are we seeking wise counsel, or are we trusting a human and their advice more than God?

I put my dad on a pedestal, and our relationship suffered because of it. Putting him in the place only God should be was expecting too much of my dad and setting him up for failure. But turning to and listening to God and asking Him to guide my earthly relationships with wisdom will allow healthy relationships to grow strong.

Remember: anything I think about or turn to more than God is what I worship.

This means anything I turn to before God, anything I crave above God, anything I listen to more than God, anyone I trust in their comfort and opinion more than God, is who or what I am worshiping. I regularly have to check what my first thought is in the mornings. What my first reaction is when something goes wrong—or even right. How many times have I received positive news and gone on about my day without thanking Him? How often have I received bad news, proceeding to worry and wallow, instead of asking for His help?

And that, my friends, is what I learned about why I have not yet seen the other side of the battlefield. I find myself running up against the same challenges because, unfortunately, learning my lesson does not always happen immediately. Many times I have to face the same challenges in different forms to continue practicing what I have learned.

Much of this happens simply because we live amongst other humans. How many times do we learn to show kindness to one person but then another shows up in our life to challenge us also? We learn spiritual endurance with each encounter, and it gets stronger the more we practice. Before long, we find ourselves unbothered by these circumstances and that is where true peace finds us! I wish this was as easy to act out as it is to write. It's not. And that is why practicing it continually is so important.

I keep starting over at the beginning because each time I endure a battle, I get stronger and stronger and keep my eyes on Him longer and longer. Sometimes, I make it through a situation with my eyes focused on Him the entire time. Sometimes, I barely make it a few steps before I look at someone or something else for comfort, which immediately halts me in my tracks and keeps me at a standstill.

I believe one day (and I am excited about that day!) I will get to Him, stay with Him, and walk out the other side to see my Father waiting for me with even more excitement than I can understand.

He will not be there tapping His foot with a frustrated look, asking, "Where have you been?!" No, He will embrace me, delighted to see me. He will dust off my ball gown and straighten my crown. (I don't believe He will require me to change my shoes because He knows I love a comfy pair of worn-in Converse over any fancy pair of shoes.)

My mom told me a story once about a friend of hers. The friend shared that in the early years of marriage, she would ride in the bench seat of her husband's truck with him and sit right in the middle, where she could be close to him. As the years passed and the newlywed phase faded, they found themselves in middle age–they also found less excitement in each other's company. One day, she sadly pondered this and shared with Him, "We used to sit together in the truck, and now we never do. What happened?" His response was simple, but deep. He said, "I haven't moved."

DRAMATIC PAUSE

Wow! Am I right? Pause worthy. Her husband had never moved; she was the one who moved.

Our Savior, who stands on top of the hill of that battlefield, has not and will not move farther from us. We move. We get farther away. We turn away. We shy away because of guilt and shame. He hasn't moved! He does not move!!

When you were a little girl, and told you had to be a "good girl" for God to love you–He never moved. But you began believing you were not acceptable to Him, so you took a few steps back.

When you were a preteen and began rebelling against the authority in your life and were told, "God would be so disappointed in you!" He never moved. You took more steps back.

By the time you reached your teenage years, you may have given your life to Christ, been baptized, and done all the things "good little Christian girls" are supposed to do. Maybe you took a few steps forward, but you still felt all that guilt and shame. The voices around you never let up, and their expectations made you feel less and less like you could ever attain what He wants. He never moved.

In your early adult years, when you gave up on traditional religion and the church, *the One who stands atop that hill did not move.* When the teachers and preachers you heard all your life only solidified the belief

ON THE OTHER SIDE OF THE BATTLEFIELD | 95

that you could never meet their seemingly indisputable expectations. And when you surrounded yourself with people who at least did not tell you that everything you do is wrong (with an occasional "who needs God anyway" thrown in). Sister, *He still never moved.*

Maybe you are still in your early adult years, or maybe, like me, you are well beyond them. Maybe we have nothing in common, or maybe we both have a few tattoos, a few relationships, and a few sips of whiskey behind us. Many people around us still think, "there is no way God will use her. There is no way she believes in Him. He will be so disappointed when she stands before Him looking like she does."

Do you want to know what I have to say? He has never moved.

He has never once run from you or me. He has never once told you He is disappointed in you, you can never return, or He will never forgive you. It is quite the opposite. In the Bible, in the book of Luke, I envision the Savior who stood on that hill telling us a story intended to show us how our Heavenly Father sees us and reacts when we are far away. I recommend reading it for yourself, but I can tell you this–God always has a plot twist. The son runs far away and spends all his money on tattoos and whiskey (okay, maybe I added that part). When he is broke, alone, and hungry, he goes back home to see if his dad will give him a job because then, at least he will have a place to live and food to eat.

So picture it. Picture yourself at your darkest, your drunkest, your highest. Picture yourself in your mugshot, amid the most degrading thing you've ever done for money, or when you were the worst mother you could have ever been. Then, picture yourself standing up, walking away, and heading across the battlefield to the One on the hill. He never moved.

96 | FEARLESSLY BECOMING

An Interesting Turn of Events

I will not pretend no one wants to see you fail. Some people will be downright angry about the turn of events that are about to catch them off guard.

In Luke, there was no battlefield. There was no Savior on the hill. There was a father at his home, missing his son. He knew his son's life had not been what he had expected. It is not the life a loving father wants for any of his children, but he can't help it. He loves him tremendously and misses him. He wants him home. Then, as he looks hopefully in the direction his son left all that time ago on the road leading away from home, he suddenly sees his son coming toward him.

Now is when he moves. He *runs.* He no longer stands, encouraging His child to come home, walk to him, and keep his eyes on him. Now is when he runs to him, scoops him up, and cries happy tears on his son's shoulder.

Friend, I hope you know there are times in life when He calls you back to where you belong. There are times in life that we must keep our eyes on Him, do the hard work, and keep moving forward. But–there comes a time when all else has failed and we have given up, thinking we are not worthy of His love. We forget we need to simply turn our head, look at Him, and take a step in His direction. That one step of obedience is when He runs with all His might to meet us and is where He will scoop us up and I imagine Him saying, "I never moved. I have waited for you all this time. I was so sad when you felt you were not enough, and I am glad you are home, my princess. Come stay with Me. Let Me protect you. Let Me take care of you. Let Me wash all the garbage away that others placed on you."

Pause and Ponder

- Have others worked to convince you that you could never come home again?
- Maybe you have been told you can never step foot in your home on this earth again–but friend, this is not our home.
- There is a place we will eventually get to on the other side of that battlefield with a mansion built specifically for you. You will be scooped up and welcomed home.
- That right there will make me want to worship the One who runs toward me, not the ones who have pushed me away.

Can I tell you again that I love you? It does not matter if we have never met. God is filling my mind with pictures of you and what it looks like for Him to run to you. You. He wants you to know He is waiting. I heard it said once that God is a gentleman and will never force His way into your life. But once you say He is welcome, He will fill your life up with all the love that He is because God IS love.

"Dear friends, let us love one another, for love comes from God. Everyone who loves has been born of God and knows God. Whoever does not love does not know God, because God is love. This is how God showed his love among us: He sent his one and only Son into the world that we might live through him. This is love: not that we loved God, but that he loved us and sent his Son as an atoning sacrifice for our sins. Dear friends, since God so loved us, we also ought to love one another. No one has ever seen God; but if we love one another, God lives in us and his love is made complete in you."—1 John 4:7-12 (NIV)[19]

I wish I could meet you face to face and tell you how much I love you, and I am sorry you were ever made to feel less than anyone in your life. I'm still on the battlefield with you, sister. But I can't do the work for you. More than anything, I want to introduce (or reintroduce) you to the One who can. He has failed no one, and He will not fail you. There are plenty of people in this world who claim to be Christians who have failed you.

The truth is, though, there are people in my life I have failed. I have been the one to hurt them and make them feel inadequate, and while I hope I never would, I might do the same to you.

I remember many times, sitting with my dad and discussing life and the battles we all face in this world. He was a man full of grace for those lost and in pain. While he will never know, I can now see that much of this book was birthed in those conversations as he taught me about loving others and offering grace for them and myself. As we would wind down these conversations, knowing we had not and would not solve anything, he would get a slight grin on his face, shake his head and say, "People are weird, man." And we are. It was the only solace we could find in the explanation of the human experience

Prayer

Father, I am one of those weird people. Yet, you made me, and there is a redemption story waiting for each of us if we simply ask You, and if we allow ourselves to trust You enough to see it. If we accept that, even amidst our weirdness, our addiction, our doubts - when others are sick and tired of listening to us–You have never given up and never left. Your goal is a relationship with us, if we will only accept it. Father, help me know that being weak is okay because it is when you offer us Your strength. I may be weird, I may be weak, I may be inconsistent and annoying... but I am Yours. Thank You that while I am still learning and growing, You are consistent and strong and will never leave. Amen

As the princess lifted her head, she saw a slight illumination in the distance. She picked herself up, determined to trudge out of the mud and head home. No matter how far, no matter how hard, she knew it was the only option left. Or she hoped it was. Would He still accept her? Would He still love her? She had to at least try, because everyone else had proven the opposite. This was her last chance before deciding to quit permanently. She stood, lifted her worn-out, mucky tennis shoe, and took a step. She had to fight through the negative thoughts, but she took another step. Suddenly, the illumination she saw off in the distance enveloped her, and her Father's arms embraced her. Once she turned to Him, He scooped her up and washed away all the muck. She was whole; she was accepted; she was loved, and she was His.

Section 2

Scripture Reading

Suggested Reading: Matthew 14: 22-33

In Section Two's suggested scripture reading, we will see what happened to Peter when he focused more on what was around him than Who was right in front of him.

I still struggle with this same thing over and over. What about you?

Do you ever feel you are rocking along pretty well with life and suddenly find yourself sinking? Welcome to being human. But more importantly, welcome to discovering someone Who will lift you instead of helping drag you down. You will see me mention the phrase "eyes on Him" multiple times throughout this book because it is the answer to so many of life's hazards.

Walking around with our heads down in constant shame cannot keep us from being tripped up by difficulties any more than our head being in the clouds can keep us from experiencing reality.

By keeping our eyes on Him, there will be no opportunity to walk in shame, judgment of others, or ignorant bliss of the world around us.

Instead, eyes on Him keeps us laser-focused on "love, joy, peace, patience, kindness, goodness, faithfulness, gentleness, and self-control." (based on Galatians 5:22-23)

A Letter to The Princess Who Never Gave Up

Well, look at you.

Girl, you messed up *a lot*. You've hurt people, you've been hurt, your first marriage didn't make it, and you really let yourself go.

Right now, you can't even imagine how soon you will be without your parents. Without that support system spiritually, emotionally, and physically. You are in defense mode, with good reason, but you don't have to be so hard.

From my view where I am now, you have lost both parents and you should have been a better daughter to them. The memories and relationships you could have had are something I regret today. But it was not all you. They, too, were people with their trauma and hangups, and sometimes life and people are simply messy. Know this: you are not more or less messy than anyone else. You are not bad, but you need to soften. I wish you had learned earlier that love and truth go hand in hand, and you do not have to protect truth at the expense of love. You do not need to feel unprotected. God has you, at this very moment, tucked tightly next to Him. You are a protected royal woman who can fight the good fight, and you can also hide behind Him when you need to. Do you want to know something that may make you mad–but makes you seem silly? You are not as tough as you think. Of course, you learned to act tough because you feel vulnerable and unprotected. You are none of those. You are not unprotected, but you are not tough, either. It is okay. You do not have to be harsh; it is okay to soften because you are strong. Remember to pull your strength from God, though. Trusting in God is powerful, and eventually, it will become a reality for you. I am sorry I did not learn this lesson sooner to protect you from all you are going through and are about to go through.

You have no idea how much better life could have been if you had stayed closer to God and prioritized your relationship with Him above everything else going on.

But, you know what? You continue to strive to improve yourself and honor God, and your parents would be proud. There is a lot more you are going to struggle through. Yet there is also a lot more to look forward to. Hint: grandkids simply make this world a brighter place.

You are okay. You are going to be okay. I am okay.

"All shall be well, and all manner of thing shall be well."

—Julian of Norwich[20]

Section 3:

Mermaids Don't Dog Paddle

Chapter 7

Mermaids Don't Dog Paddle

"Forget the former things; do not dwell on the past. See, I am doing a new thing! Now it springs up; do you not perceive it? I am making a way in the wilderness and streams in the wasteland." —Isaiah 43:18-19 (NIV)[21]

    Castles in the distance with homes and gathering places in the forefront. All bustling with the busyness of any typical small community. Everyone stops to say hi to one another as they pass by; this is a different busyness than you would see in a large city. This small town is busy with a few groups of people milling about the neighborhood, talking and waving as they pass. A few others, a bit more quick-paced, pass by in the street, excited to get to their destination. Some look out their windows at those below, and a baby is even being pushed in a stroller of sorts. It is quiet and serene. There is an air of intentionality, but no rush.

Can you even rush while underwater? (Raise your hand if you knew mermaid kingdoms even existed!) It was baffling to me, at first, that God would use this visual to teach me a lesson. But He is often a God of the unexpected. Anyway, everything seems to move at a slower pace underwater, does it not? Peace, I believe, is the word I am looking for. Not slow, but at a peaceful rhythm that can soothe a soul once it quits trying to fight its way back to land.

How intriguing to watch! A community of mermaids going about mermaid business with their mermaid families, neighbors, and friends. The distant castle turrets are detailed with beautifully carved designs while underwater flora and fauna drift about. Some sort of climbing flora decorates the sides of the castles, much like ivy would on dry land. The yards are bright with plants which seem intentionally placed. I never thought about it before, but I suppose even mermaids garden. Well, since these are castles, maybe they have gardeners? I didn't think to ask, distracted by the sunlight sparkling throughout the entire area in a uniquely broken-prism way, only capable of happening underwater.

And life simply flows in the rhythm of peace.

Pause and Ponder

- Can you picture the scene above? Maybe it reminds you of a book or a movie, or maybe you can visually create your own scene. The main thing I want to make sure you note is the peace.
- How much peace do you have right now in your life?
- Do you know specifically which areas of your life bring peace and which do not?

The Tipping Point

The mermaid story came from an experience I had a short time after my mom died. We had lost my dad unexpectedly only three years prior, and my mom was there, seemingly healthy one day, and not the next. It was too much; the grief hit so violently it knocked me off-kilter and kept me that way for quite a while. I deal with emergencies pretty well—for the most part. I can stay calm and in control, handling what needs to be handled until everyone else is taken care of. Then, once things settle, I am hit with a season of anxiety or depression as I finally process the situation. This time was different. The violent grief hit hard, and it hit fast, and it lasted for much longer than I expected. At the time of this story, most would say the dust had settled because the funeral had long come and gone, and all the matters that come along with the death of both parents were finally taken care of. Life was going about its normal self... but I was not.

Pause and Ponder

- I want to take a moment here and acknowledge you. If we could chat, I would tell you I recognize your pain; I can see it in your eyes. While I can't do that now, can I tell you this? I see it in your spirit. The heaviness I feel as I write tells me you are hurting and need to know you are not being ignored. If I can sense your hurt, how much more can God laser focus on you, His heir, His favored royal child?
- Remind yourself of what we have already discussed: you are His, you are royal, and you are not just another one in an enormous group of people who believe in Him. He can pick you out in a crowd or find you in your deepest hidden

places. His eyes are trained to know you and your gestures and posture and to recognize you like no other can.

- The battle you are in has not left you so broken that you are unrecognizable to Him, no matter what anyone else says. He. Sees. YOU.

Why Are You Trying to Keep Your Head Above Water?

I finally was at my breaking point, and I remember screaming internally, **"I CANNOT KEEP MY HEAD ABOVE WATER ANYMORE! I CAN'T KEEP DOG PADDLING LIKE THIS!"** Inside my head, yet from a different space, I hear a soft voice ask, "Why are you trying to keep your head above water?" Honestly, it made me angry. **"WHAT DO YOU WANT ME TO DO, DROWN?"** In that instant, that different little space in my mind showed me a view of the story I wrote above, a little movie playing in my mind of an underwater kingdom. The peace filled me, and He showed me all I was trying so desperately to hold on to was dull, lifeless, and second best. He had so much more to show me if I would just quit trying to keep my head in this limited and dreary place and finally embrace where He intended for me to be all along.

For me, trusting in Him is letting go of the expectations I (and others) have for me—and knowing He has a better adventure than my imagination could ever dream up. I simply have to quit trying to keep my head above water and let Him show me a new way of thriving.

Pause and Ponder

- Are you also holding on too hard to a place where you do not belong?

- Can you see we are discussing a spiritual place more than a physical one?
- What untruths have you been told in the past that you need to let go of now? What situation is keeping you drained, and you need God to intervene?

Learning to Swim in the Rhythms of Grace

God, my gentle and kind Father, took me on a journey over this season of life that taught me I was trying to live the way I saw others doing and the way they expected me to. People all around me seem to thrive in this world where there is a set expectation of how we are intended to be. Of course, we know there are fads in life, some we quickly grab hold of and those we can easily ignore, yet what He began showing me was so much more than that. He began showing me the trends that were years in the making, such as:

- Being in a perpetual state of rushing
- The church is a place of condemnation and formality
- Anxiety and depression are a common norm
- Overworking is a status symbol
- Picture-perfect homes packed full of accumulated items and fashionable decor
- Overconsumption: we buy too much, eat too much, drink too much, watch too much, and listen to too many people
- Lack of peace

Honestly, I could go on and on with this list, and it would only scratch the surface of how we have let a generation of trends (not a small season of trends) take over our lives. When we become intentional

MERMAIDS DON'T DOG PADDLE | 113

about our personal relationship with God, we see the areas we have allowed others to influence us—many times, to our detriment. On top of that, many of us are conquering enormous giants like lack of affection in our families, and some are breaking cycles of abuse. These are noble and imperative quests! And quite exhausting! If you are one of those determined to no longer continue in the habitual negativity passed down, then let me say again, *girl, God sees you!* And I honestly believe He is so proud of you!

On top of that, I want to say He also has rest for your weary soul. Remember the battle we talked about earlier in this book? I want us to consider that, along with doing the hard work of being a cycle breaker, He does not leave us alone and exhausted.

Let's think beyond our immediate families and zoom out. Do you remember when we looked at timelines in history class? Let's zoom out to a level beyond a few years and the smallness of our family or local area, and look at a generation as a whole. Ours is but a blip on the timeline, yet filled with unrest, chaos, anxiety, and addictions to everything from working too much to watching too much television to overeating or consuming some other substance to fill voids and make us forget. Let's move back down the timeline a generation or so to a time before the busyness and pressures of today. Just a generation ago, we did not have the technological distractions we now have. Going outside and entertaining ourselves was expected, not an option. Fast food was just beginning to be normal, but it was an occasional treat, not a normal meal because we were too busy and tired to cook.

A few brief blips on the timeline before was a generation traveling by horse and buggy; writing a letter was the only communication other than speaking to them directly. Church was the main social activity of the week, and there was little reason to be inside unless it was raining or too cold.

We could go on and on, but the point I'm trying to make is that while we have many great advancements that help us today (I like to say if Caroline Ingalls from the classic television series, Little House on the Prairie, was gifted with an electric mixer, I highly doubt she would have refused it), we also are so busy and chaotic that we never slow down. We never rest from work. Or, on the flip side, we become so complacent or overwhelmed we get still–too still. We sit for hours, scrolling or binge-watching to quiet the expectations that overwhelm us.

What God showed me through the beautiful mermaid kingdom was it is okay to have peace in our life. To slow down enough to enjoy the people and scenery around you. Before you think, "I don't even like the people around me," "Have you seen where I live?" or anything else along those lines, let me tell you this. Seriously, I hear you. I have thought many of the same things, and I believe it is exactly why He showed me that place. He showed me I was fighting hard to stay in a place not meant for me. I was trying to fit into crowds and lifestyles not meant for me. Losing both my parents catapulted me onto a path of removing myself from pretty much everyone and everything. While it seemed at the time I was cold or dealing in an unhealthy way, what happened was a season of creating fewer expectations in my life. I could not meet the demands and expectations the people in my life were accustomed to from me. I was done. Emotionally, mentally, physically, and almost spiritually, done.

I will also note during this time, I had two surgeries, lots of personal and relational turmoil, and a draining job. I was spending less and less time with God, but more and more time being busy trying to act like a perfect Christian. Losing my parents was simply the major catalyst for change in a season already beginning to crash and burn.

MERMAIDS DON'T DOG PADDLE | 115

Pause and Ponder

- What kind of season are you in? Do you relate to what I was going through, or are you in a season of peace?
- What area of life would you say you are ready to see the most change? Or, if you were like me, is it every part?
- In a perfect world, without putting the limitations of the expectations of this generation on yourself, what would your life look like?
- (Before you answer this question, please allow yourself to think about it sincerely. Simmer in it for a few moments or days if needed.) Are you willing to let God show you a new way of life that could completely upend where you are or even leave you in the exact situation you are currently in?

If your honest answer to the last question is 'no', can I encourage you that God will not be mad at you? An honest no is much better than a yes when you lie to yourself and Him. Being honest with God gives you the opportunity for the beginning of a truly authentic relationship with Him.

I heard someone say if you are struggling with an action you desperately want to change but can't, maybe it is time to quit focusing on the action and begin focusing your prayers to find the desire to quit. Good grief, that resonated with me. Sometimes I want to stop doing something, but do I? Yes. I do. But then again, I don't. So, instead of focusing on the fact I keep doing whatever it is, I need to ask God to show me why I'm reluctant to give it up. What is in me that is fighting so badly? So my prayer is, slowly but surely, He changes me in a way that I will want to give the action up; to understand what purpose the action is serving and to allow Him to fill the need in other ways. This, my friends, is a work in progress.

While the mermaid kingdom was a beautiful visual of where He was taking me, it was not an instant journey. I was hoping for a teleportation travel plan that was quick and painless, but it was not what I needed. He knew and had a much better travel plan for my future.

"If I find in myself a desire which no experience in this world can satisfy, the most probable explanation is that I was made for another world."
—CS Lewis[22]

Prayer

Father, You did it again. You showed me all I have been holding onto and putting my faith in is worthless. You showed me the life I have been clinging to desperately is not what YOU expect of me. I felt like I was letting everyone down, especially You, if I stepped back from all the responsibilities and expectations. On the contrary, what I found when I stepped back was You. I felt as if I had been chasing You. Chasing Your approval and acceptance when, as You showed me on the battlefield, You never moved. When I quit running and trying to act like a good Christian girl, I found You... or should I say, where You led me. And honestly, I never want to go back.

Thank You.

The princess, who we have already established, is unique, realized she had settled into a world that was all wrong for her. The King showed her the kingdom He had prepared for her, where her talents and skills were needed, and her personality was embraced. She suddenly realized how exhausted she was, not from trying to do all He called her to, but from trying to force all He called her to on the wrong people in the wrong places. She tells others, "Whatever it is you expect the King to bring will pale in comparison to what He shows up with. He always shows up with more than we could ever imagine." He proved her right once again.

Chapter 8

A New Place to Live

"I have told you these things, so that in me you may have peace. In this world you will have trouble. But take heart! I have overcome the world."
—1 John 16:33 (NIV)[23]

Here I was with the vision and understanding that I was not where I was intended to be. My physical circumstances were not the issue; it was my emotional and spiritual situation that needed the most work. And guess who was responsible for all of that? Yep, me. I could have said (and believe me, I tried many times), "If only I had a different job or spouse. If only I had better parents, teachers, or friends." I have watched so many people 'start over' or try to get a new life in some way, which can be an irresistible temptation! Since I was a little girl, I've dreamed one day I would jump in the car and fill the tank with gas, and whatever town I ended up in is where I would start a new life. I had this idea in my head that I would drain that tank dry and drive until I ended up in some quaint little New England town where no one knew me, but everyone would immediately embrace me. Y'all, I live in the middle of nowhere Texas. I used to commute one hour one way to work. Driving until I ran out of gas will not get me far, and it certainly won't get me to New England. A new plan had to emerge. I realized (after much whining and deflecting) that the people in my life were not the issue. I was.

Pause and Ponder

- Do you wish you could run away?
- Do you recognize the role you play? As an adult, I realized wherever I go, the problems will go with me because I will still be there. It's not a THEM issue; it's a ME issue. The following quote sums this idea up well:
  *"So, the cross is always ready and waits for you everywhere. You cannot escape it no matter where you run, for wherever you go, you are burdened with yourself. **Wherever you go, there you are.**"* —Thomas a Kempis, Imitation of Christ, ca. A.D. 1440[24]
- Are you ready to differentiate your role from those others play in your life?

Tell Your Hurts to Grow Up

Remember when I said that one of my current favorite quotes is, "We are all just walking each other home?" I randomly saw this quote online, and God used it to inspire me. But this was a time in my life when I began looking at all I was doing, all I was giving my time to, and all I believed about myself and God. If I was not where I was supposed to be, then where was I, and where was it I should be instead? I began reflecting and asking myself and God, *'Why?'* Why am I involved in this activity? Why do I read my Bible? What do I truly believe? Why do I listen to certain people? Why do I let the behavior of others affect me so much? Why do I have to stay in a job I'm unfulfilled in? Why did I lose my parents when I needed them so terribly? Why is life so difficult? Why do good things happen to bad people? And on and on and on.

During my preteen years, the constant chorus of, "You're too much," rang in my ears, as it was spoken over me countless times by people in my life. It seemed I was either too quiet or too loud, I laughed too often or I was too serious, I worried too much or I was thoughtless. I was criticized for eating too much, feeling too deeply, and for my unique taste in certain styles and interests. Then, on a particular day forever etched in my memory, I reached a breaking point. I thought, "If I'm always 'too much' for everyone, regardless of what I do, and if they keep complaining no matter how I behave, then I will not show my emotions to anyone anymore."

I grew up in a time when disagreeing with adults equated to being rude or disrespectful, which made it challenging for kids to express their individuality or emotions. Kids were taught to remain silent and comply with authority without question. When we got upset about something, we were not allowed to express our emotions. We were expected to agree and be happy about it—whatever *it* was. So, I determined if I was not allowed to express my disappointments, I would also refrain from expressing my happiness. If others thought I was too silly and laughed too much, I would not show joy or sadness. I chose to try and show no emotion. It was the only way I knew to gain control of what felt to be zero control in my life.

A NEW PLACE TO LIVE | 123

A life coach once asked me, "Okay, how has that served you?" I responded, "Very well, actually," because it has protected me from much disappointment and frustration. He asked, "Okay, how has it served you in relationships?" I wanted to tell him to shut up because it forced me to admit it was utterly destructive in pretty much every relationship in my life. I would begin a relationship of any kind with the hope I could be me, fully me. But at even the tiniest indication they thought I was 'too' something, I would completely shut down. I would sever the relationship entirely, or at least keep from getting any closer. Many of my relationships, even if they still exist today, have stayed frozen in that state.

Once I recognized how detrimental this had been, the life coach walked me through a process of thinking back to what created the situation and determining how I would have handled it if it happened to me now as a grown adult with better coping skills. He shared I could then choose what is best for myself and the relationships I have or will develop. He was helping me see I could quit reacting like the scared little girl who internalized every situation, and I could understand we are all just *walking each other home* and other people make mistakes just as I do—and it is not a personal attack on me. Maybe they, too, are reacting like the scared and fragile preteens or toddlers who did whatever they had to do to protect themselves.

In my current relationships, I try to handle offenses with the lessons learned from my life coach in mind. I've realized it's often less about me and more about the other person's struggles when they act hurtfully. So, I've chosen to respond rather than react. I take a moment to pray and process things with a mix of logic and love. What's impressive is many of these relationships, ones I'd usually have walked away from, have grown stronger and deeper. I've also received grace in places where I did not believe I deserved it. When we extend grace, we often end up receiving it in return. It might not happen instantly or in the way we expect, but eventually, we will look back and see how God's grace made a significant difference in our lives.

Pause and Ponder

- Do you ever find yourself in a season of questioning? Are you currently in one?
- Think about, or write, some questions you are struggling with.
- Have you found yourself responding in old ways, even though you have long been outside the situation where you developed that coping technique?
- Are you currently in a situation making you need to defend yourself and you are not sure how to respond?
- Now, you have to make a hard decision. Will you take responsibility for your reactions and do what it takes to correct them, if possible?

Respond, Not React

A piece of advice my father gave me was, "Never react. You can respond, but never react." This advice has been a staple in my life, and I have worked hard to act on this advice. I don't always get it right, but I always strive to do so. You see, when we react, it is impulsive and without thought. When we respond, it is controlled, thought out, prayed over, and logical. This does not mean we must wait five to seven business days to respond to an offense. It means instead of an impulsive reaction we may regret later, we take a beat, put our mind on God, say a

A NEW PLACE TO LIVE | 125

quick prayer asking Him to give us wisdom and restraint, and respond in truth and love to the best of our ability. (And yes, sometimes this means not responding at all.) You can respond with a phrase like:

- "I need time to process what you said, so I will go for a walk and pray about my response."
- "I choose not to make this worse by reacting."
- "I love you too much to react right now."
- "Our relationship is more important to me than this argument, so I will not react to that statement/action."
- "That hurt me, and I love you too much to retaliate, but we will need to discuss this once we can calm down."

There are infinite ways to quickly respond, diffuse the situation, and end the conversation without conceding or giving in and feeling defeated. Is it easy? Of course not. We want to defend ourselves. We want to retaliate. What we want at the moment is to make them pay for how they treated us. When we truly stop and think about it, it is probably not what we want in the long run.

The choice to walk in God's strength through any situation is where true power comes from. I am not saying He will give you supernatural strength to overcome and move on, and you will never be bothered by hurts again. What I'm saying is staying tucked tightly close to Him and allowing Him to fight your battles while you choose peace is where the transformation happens.

Pause and Ponder

- Can you see the difference in taking responsibility for yourself without taking blame?

- Learning to respond vs. react helps you regain the balance needed in difficult situations.
- Sometimes, we are taught incorrect beliefs, dismissed, abused, and more. There is power in taking responsibility for our response because we can make powerful decisions to stop the actions.
- Pray for wisdom and remember reading scripture for ourselves is imperative to breaking the chains others have kept us entangled in.
- Be sure when reading scripture you read what it says and not what you've been told it says. Never depend on someone else to be your sole source of knowledge. Jesus died to give us direct access; let's not waste that.

What Does Any of This Have To Do With Mermaids?

In the section above, I shared the phrase "while you choose peace," and peace is exactly the place I was supposed to be. Instead, I resided in a land of chaos, turmoil, and frustration. I was trying so hard to act acceptably and keep up the appearance I felt was expected of me–and I expected those around me to do the same. The new world God wanted to show me was a world of peace. What's amazing is that nothing about my situation had to change for me to find peace. God reminded me of the steps we discussed in this chapter (listed below), and they led me to peace.

Now, when peace is compromised, it is obvious to me, and I can begin following these critical, life-changing steps:

1. Quit trying to dog-paddle in a puddle of chaos when peace is waiting for me.

2. Recognize I can't force others to live in peace, and they also can't force me to live outside of it.

3. Recognize what past hurts are activated, keeping me defensive or shut down, and process them as an adult.

4. Begin intentionally responding as opposed to reacting.

5. Thank God that His peace is attainable.

Prayer

Jehovah Jireh, thank You for Your almighty provision and protection! I pray we understand the grace You offer us so we can, in turn, offer it to others. I do not deserve any forgiveness You show me, yet I struggle to forgive others. Yes, people have wronged me, but no more than I have wronged others. I can only give someone what I have been given, and You have blessed me with a huge amount of forgiveness so I can pass it on. It's hard, Father; help my weakness and give me a heart of forgiveness accompanied by Your strength. Forgiving does not mean we must allow wrong actions to continue. But we can respond, not react, and use wisdom to make decisions that protect ourselves. I am grateful You do not tell us to stay in harmful situations, although we are often told we should. Safety: spiritual, physical, or emotional, shouldn't be a luxury. We can trust You and seek safety and wise counsel simultaneously.

Beat down in body, mind, and soul, the princess learned no one else could dictate her relationship with her King. He called her Daughter, lifted her to a new way of life, and gave her access to His direct line. At any moment, with only an ask, He will speak life-giving words and powerful strength-building scriptures over her. He will sing songs of peace and love to His princess, who so often gets turned around in the kingdom, losing her way back home. Yet with one turn toward Him, He never tires of lifting her into His arms and tucking her tight into bed to rest in the peace only true home can offer.

Chapter 9

Acting vs. Being

"For I know that good itself does not dwell in me, that is, in my sinful nature. For I have the desire to do what is good, but I cannot carry it out. For I do not do the good I want to do, but the evil I do not want to do—this I keep on doing." —Romans 7:18-19 (NIV)[25]

As a child, I was taught to 'act' as a child should—not necessarily through the Word of God, but through man's skewed interpretation. Through this faulty lens, I was taught what scripture says about God's expectations for my life. Still, there is a difference between understanding a subject while embracing it as a moral choice and simply doing what people expected from me to appear the way they believed was correct.

A few years ago, God reminded me there is a difference between acting and being. Do I want to simply *act* like others deemed the ideal Christian should? Do I want to act like I love people and love learning and following scripture, or do I want to truly love people and love learning God's Word and following what I learn from scripture? There is a big difference between the two that I had never seen before.

Growing up and into adulthood, I worked hard at acting as others expected me to, not rocking the boat too much, performing acts of kindness, and so on. Much of what I did was because it was expected of me. Yet there was another part of me that sensed some of what others were teaching actually had some merit. These are the aspects found in scripture that line up with what the scriptures teach us to do. I knew I believed the scripture and wanted to become who it says I should become. When God posed those questions to me of acting vs. being, it caused a shaking in me. It woke me up to truth through His perspective because, in all my childhood and adult years, I convinced myself I was living as I should. Of course, I knew I was not perfect. But for the most part, I was going to church, trying to treat people well, and trying to have a relationship with God.

In true God fashion, He gently began showing me areas in my life where I was still *acting*, and to my surprise, it was pretty much every aspect of my life. As a mother, I was *acting* as I believed a mom should. I loved being a mother and wanted to excel at it because I enjoyed and loved my daughter so much. My daughter was such a beautiful, sweet, and fun kid, and I wanted to be the mom I knew she deserved. So, to the best of my ability, I attempted to be that mom. As a wife, I wanted to be the *ideal* wife, taking care of the family and home in the way I believed was best. There I was again, *acting* like a wife and homemaker, according to the idea I had in my head. As one in the community, I wanted to be a giving, loving person to people in the community and church. So, I *acted* the way I thought a giving, loving person should.

For most of my life, things went according to plan by utilizing this script. I showed only the side of myself I wanted people to see. Unfortunately, the realities of what was happening inside me, my home, and other close relationships were not so positive. I was disappointed in myself that there was a disconnect between what I wanted to do, what I showed others I did, and what was occurring. I didn't understand what was wrong, because as far as I knew, I was simply working to meet expectations. I had a deeply ingrained misconception of scripture fighting against me. I could somehow meet all expectations I felt others had for me, then the promises of God would follow.

Over time, I realized no one was falling for my act. The people in my life could see I was depressed, self-loathing, angry, anxious, condemning, and harsh to others. It was obvious that I was never satisfied with myself or anyone else. So, while trying to be the perfect wife and mother, I was instead accomplishing the opposite. I believe many others are caught in this same trap, for Scripture does not tell us to *act*. It tells us to *be* Christ-like. Growing up under such spiritual confusion surrounding this, I found it nearly impossible to differentiate the two. I believed they were the same.

For example, how often do you see a social issue we know is not how scripture tells us to behave, so Christians decide to berate, belittle, and correct—all in the name of being a perfect Christian? Instead, we should respond rather than react. We could take a beat and read more than one scripture about a subject. We could study how God, Jesus, and the Holy Spirit taught us to respond in similar situations. Then, we can be an example of what is correct and invite others to walk the path home with us. The problem many people see with this is that a quick reaction evokes a much more potent and immediate action. Unfortunately, that action tends to be out of fear, embarrassment, or anger, and the cycle continues over and over.

The method of responding with calmness can sometimes require us to develop relationships with people we disagree with; we invite people on our journey, and walk and talk, or join them on their journey. Not in

ACTING VS. BEING | 135

such a way that we join in on what we disagree with, but that we get to know a person and where they are coming from. It can be a longer, more disciplined process than simply spewing an immediate reaction. It is also the process of being instead of acting, where we are less interested in the public show of spewing so-called 'Christianity,' and we are much more involved in the true heart behind helping others on their journey to Him.

Once He showed me the difference between acting and being, I have never been the same. I am far from perfecting it, but this practice permeates deeply and convicts me strongly when I try to ignore how He taught me to focus on being true to Him, no matter how that appears to others. Now I have a loving example of how to help myself simply be the person I always thought I was. I am much less concerned about what people think of me and much more concerned about what they think of Him–*Jesus*. Being a Christian who spews reactions that spread discord does not exemplify the truth of who God is. I don't merely want to act like Him. I want to truly be different and be an example of Him to others. Modeling His loving nature and grace-filled character to those in my life.

Pause and Ponder

- Is acting vs. being new to you as it was to me?
- If it's not a new concept, are you willing to take some time and evaluate the truest reason behind how you act?
- Are you ready to pray and ask God to reveal to you if there are situations in your life where you are still putting on an act? I can tell you I see this happen a lot within the church. We can become so busy volunteering and being helpers that it quickly becomes something we do out of expectation

instead of a genuine act of service. The same holds in many other relationships as well.

Don't Be That Person

Let's take a moment to reflect on how far we've come in our time together throughout the pages of this book. In Section 1, we learned we may not see ourselves the way He does, and possibly taught we could not be good enough for Him. It's easy to believe God would never accept someone with the flaws we have and the sins we have committed. People may say things about us that don't line up with how a princess should look or act, so we assume He also could never see us in such a way. We have bought into the lie that if we aren't pleasing people, then we aren't pleasing Him. If we don't fit their mold, then He couldn't possibly accept us either.

Then we fought the battle in Section 2 of the book; seeing that we were trying to do it all on our own without relying on Him. Believing if we met certain expectations as Christians, we would have the faith and discipline to stand strong on our own and overcome evil. We may deal with being too proud to ask for help or may have been shown repeatedly by others in our lives that speaking about a struggle or asking for help during a struggle may mean we don't have enough faith. We believe a strong Christian should be able to overcome by digging in our heels. Yet, we saw God calling us to Himself to recognize He has already fought for us and does not expect us to conquer everything on our own.

In my life, I have learned that recognizing my weakness keeps me focused and dependent on Him. But for most of my life, I operated under the misguided belief that my faith must not be strong enough if I am still dealing with hardships. My friend, please hear me say this:

ACTING VS. BEING | 137

There is a fine line between standing strong in faith and trying to do it all in your power. Many people wobble back and forth on this line and are confused. Remember who you are—a chosen, beautiful, treasured daughter of God—God loves you, flaws and all.

In Section 3, we saw there is an alternative path, there is a new world where we are being called to bring peace. It is the place we exist, surrounded by the Holy Spirit guiding us and the events going on around us. No matter how chaotic and difficult our situations are, we can move in peace and in the authenticity of who we are, without having to try so hard to belong somewhere we do not. When we stop trying to fit, we realize where we truly belong: in a rich, meaningful relationship with our Heavenly Father. The more we focus on that, the more all else seems to find a natural and peaceful path to Him.

I believe our culture lives on this bizarre, crazy wheel where we end up treating people who don't agree with us poorly. When the wheel turns, we end up on the receiving end of poor treatment, as they treat us the way we taught them to treat someone they disagree with–and the entire cycle continues revolving around and around this mass of unforgiveness. Friend, I have stepped off the crazy wheel to step into the new kingdom of peace God has created for His royal family to live in while here on this earth. And pray I can take many people by the hand and invite them to walk home, to Him, with me.

". . . all shall be well, and all shall be well and all manner of thing shall be well,"--Julian of Norwich20

My friend, we did it! We finished this book hand in hand as sisters and hand in hand with our Heavenly Father. I have cried, whined, and given up so many times–but God was always faithful to wipe my tears, call me out, and help me up. This book is His to use and do with as He sees fit. I pray it has been a deep blessing to you, my reader, as you are the one I have pictured as I've written and wept over the pages in this book. You, the humble princess, who may have felt lost at times, can look up and see the Father smiling down and wiping your tears.

Most importantly, I pray you raise your hands in worship from the mud, from the alley, from the bar, from the depression bed, from the grips of anxiety, from the overwhelm of motherhood, from the pit of despair, from the sadness of unmet expectations, from your dealer's driveway, from your hate-filled mind, and realize how much Jesus loves you. Right here, right now, just as you are. He smiles over you today and accepts you into His loving arms. Will you run to Him today? Will you fall to your knees in surrender, knowing how deeply loved and valued you are, while accepting what you've been taught throughout your life may not be true? But Truth has a name, and it's Jesus. He awaits with arms of love to walk you through His Word and teach you right from His heart. You are His princess.

Prayer

Thank You, Father, for the love you have poured out on me through this journey! Thank You for the crown that sits atop my head. That's what You see when You look at me. Help me see it as well. Thank You I can have my unique "ball gown." It may be glittery and flowing, or it may be sweatpants and a concert t-shirt—You love me just the same! You made me unique. I was not created to look and act like any other except the me You planned for. Help me find the peace and joy that comes from being the person You imagined as You formed me in my mother's womb. You are my Father, and I am Your child.

I love You. Amen.

The princess learned who she was. She girded her faith and made it through the battlefield into the arms of her King, understanding He was all she needed to make it through anything that came her way. She learned a new world of peace was waiting for her; a world that had a Prince determined to walk with her every step of the way as she continued her journey home. Her new goals were: Book open, eyes on Him, return crowns to their rightful owners, and walk home into the arms of her waiting King with as many others as she could.

Section 3

Scripture Reading

Sit With the King

Suggested Reading: Ephesians 1 & 2

Ephesians 1 & 2 are short, awesomely transformational chapters!! These chapters are where Paul, an apostle of Christ, teaches us who we are in Christ. I have to say; I find it hard to know which scripture pertains to all of us as Christians and which ones pertain to only specific people at a point in time.

These scriptures, however, are direct to believers. While yes, they were written to a specific church; they were written to them as believers, and it seems they could have gone to any church, even ours.

In these chapters, we read promises such as:

"And you also were included in Christ when you heard the message of truth, the gospel of your salvation. When you believed, you were marked in him with a seal, the promised Holy Spirit, who *is a deposit guaranteeing our inheritance until the redemption of those who are God's possession—to the praise of his glory."* Ephesians: 1: 13-14 (NIV)[26]

I can think of no better way than to do a practice which was shown in the movie Overcomer. The characters read through Ephesians 1 & 2 and listed everything in the chapters God says about us or has done for us.

Statements such as

- Has blessed us in heavenly realms with every spiritual blessing (Chapter 1, vs 3)
- He chose us (Chapter 1, vs 4)

There is no proper way to do this. My favorite way to learn from God is to sit with Him as I would a friend and talk. As you do, listen to the voice in your thoughts, listen to your 'gut,' your 'instinct,' and your conscience. The Holy Spirit is likely speaking to you. His Spirit, combined with His Word, is a recipe for a beautiful conversation.

Tip: Practice makes progress! If it seems odd to sit and speak and listen, it is okay. Just as with any other activity, practicing makes us more comfortable and skilled. For most of us, the earth doesn't shake and we don't always have a physical or emotional reaction when we hear from Him.

He replied, "I have been very zealous for the LORD God Almighty. The Israelites have rejected your covenant, torn down your altars, and put your prophets to death with the sword. I am the only one left, and now they are trying to kill me too." The LORD said, "Go out and stand on the mountain in the presence of the LORD, for the LORD is about to pass by." Then a great and powerful wind tore the mountains apart and shattered the rocks before the LORD, but the LORD was not in the wind. After the wind, there was an earthquake, but the LORD was not in the earthquake. After the earthquake came a fire, but the Lord was not in the fire. And after the fire came a gentle whisper. When Elijah heard it, he pulled his cloak over his face and went out and stood at the mouth of the cave. Then a voice said to him, *What are you doing here, Elijah?"* 1 Kings 19: 11-13 (NIV)[27]

Elijah was a great man of God, and God showed even Elijah to look for Him in the still, small voice. You are His beloved princess, and He will come to you with that same still, small voice. It does not matter if you are a delicate little flower, or the toughest chick to ever exist. He will still reach down to gently hold you in the palm of His hand and speak gentle, healing words over you. Because He sees you as worthy. Because you believe in His son, you are worthy. Because He has chosen to love you, you are worthy.

Sister, I hope you have found your crown, shined it up, and put it back where it belongs. He handcrafted your crown, in your style, to fit only you. It is not a duplicate of any other, its style does not suit someone else better. I spent too many years attempting to be the good little church girl instead of the tattooed princess I longed to be. You don't have to. You also do not have to be a tough, thick-skinned, carrying-too-much momma. Lay all of it down and be the soft-spoken, tutu-wearing little girl screaming inside of you to be noticed. His Spirit has a way of melting off all the acting and the costumes we have worn for so long. Let Him.

SECTION 3: MERMAIDS DON'T DOG PADDLE | 145

Conclusion

After her adoption, many hard-fought battles, and even a tumultuous time at sea–the princess found peace in the only place it can truly be found– her Father, The King. He loved her wildly, fiercely, and deeply, and she committed to do the same for those around her who are still unaware of their own adoption into royalty.

Sister, let's walk home together, and introduce as many as we can to our Father along the way. Tighten up your laces, dust off your crown, and pick up your sword. We have a journey to make.

"When they saw him, they worshiped him; but some doubted. Then Jesus came to them and said, 'All authority in heaven and on earth has been given to me. Therefore go and make disciples of all nations, baptizing them in the name of the Father and of the Son and of the Holy Spirit, and teaching them to obey everything I have commanded you. And surely I am with you always, to the very end of the age.'"-- Matthew 28:17-20 (NIV)[28]

Acknowledgments

God said "Write," and I asked a million questions. To this day, He continues to give me that one word. I pray this book honors His command, which actually was more of an invitation to a journey as a Father/daughter duo. I quickly learned that what I believed was a Father/daughter project ended up including many other women (and a couple men) which He invited along for this journey also–and what a beautiful, stretching journey it has been.

Fearlessly Unbecoming is my hope for the current and future generations of women in my family and yours.

To everyone who had a part–It's done! Your hard work and mine has finally found its natural conclusion to this journey. Without you I would still be sitting on the side of the road waiting for a roadmap. Thank you for helping guide me along the way.

My husband, Jonathan, has always made sure that I have what I need to write to my heart's content and never once failed to encourage me–although there may have been a loving eye roll or two as I doubted myself from time to time. He has stood beside me from the first moment I shared that God said "write" and listen as I wrestled with each step–he deserves an award.

Ben and Bonnie have always questioned why I questioned myself. Their confidence in me being me has shocked me and brought perspective when I needed it most. Bonnie, I hope you find yourself in these pages and know how loved and adored you are. Ben, thank you for always being the one I can talk out my wildest thoughts and what ifs with. Those conversations help keep the imagination and creativity stirring.

Sisterhood brings life lessons that challenge and grow you like none other. Sissy, you have called me out when needed and helped me remember that doubting God's ability to love and see me is ridiculous. You never hesitate to remind me who He is and I thank you for that more than I can say. I know you know how imperative it is to remember. And by the way–I have finally figured out that neither of us are driving– He is–thank goodness!

Hannah, you are and have always been my sunshine. Everything I have "unbecome" is to be a better version of me for you. You are the woman I wish I could have been at your age and you continue to impress with each year. I will forever hope you dance. Vivianne, my Princess Buttercup, may you fearlessly grow to fulfill the desires God places within your heart. My prayer is you never need to "unbecome," but should you find that you must—do it fearlessly, without apology, and all to the glory of God! Should any more princesses come along, know this. You are loved wildly, fiercely, and deeply. You deserve your Prince but remember He sits beside the King of Kings and cannot be replaced with anything or anyone of this world.

Lisa, as a friend from the beginning of time (or so it seems) I am honored that you took the time to proof this book. Your unfailing commitment to keeping me focused on the opinion of the only One who matters is a gift I can only hope to give back to you when the time is right. You are a joy!

Niki and Shelby, you have done nothing short of insist that I finish this project. Your encouragement, handholding, and gentle kicks occasionally are why this book has become a completed manuscript.

Thank you is not nearly enough to express what I want to say to you two. To go from not having a table I felt comfortable at to sitting with you at a table The Father created for us has been a surprise and blessing that I never would have guessed. May you never doubt your impact on this dull world and may your crowns sit effortlessly atop your head for all to see. Niki, your relational style of editing was exactly what I needed to put my fears aside knowing your heart was to guard my story as if it were your own and help me finalize it with confidence. Thank you for that.

Krissy Nelson has coached me through this process and helped me go from the idea to the finished product—which I doubted was even possible. Her obedience to His calling helped my obedience become a reality. Shonda Ramsey has beautifully designed and formatted this book. She quickly became a friend and helped guide me far above and beyond what her role would ever call for. I can say this book is a physical reality because these two women honored Him with their gifts and I was blessed to be a part. Tj Ray was the first editor and only male to get his hands on this book. I am grateful for his professionalism, his perspective and his kindness for this newbie, who was terrified to hand it over.

Last, but not least—the soundtrack of the last year which has served me faithfully to help me focus while writing and keep my eyes on the King of Kings was the Josh Snodgrass album labeled *Worship Guitar.* His worship guitar music was the perfect backdrop whether I was writing, reading scripture, or talking with my Father. Thank you Josh for sharing your gifts with the rest of us!

I believe that obedience is God's love language and while my obedience has been a long time coming with this specific project. I pray He accepts my feeble gift and that my response time to His next invitation be instantaneous.

ACKNOWLEDGEMNTS | 151

About the Author

Tami J Gray is a serial creative who has paired her creativity with her love of problem-solving and technical curiosity to create The Gray Factor, LLC. Her business lifeblood is walking alongside female entrepreneurs who have giants to slay and adventures to focus on without being slowed down by the valuable yet technical aspects that try to split their attention. Tami's mix of creative and analytical styles has a unique ability to take the ideas of an entrepreneur and put them into practice in logical and easily replicable forms for future success. Her goal is to help other authors by taking care of behind the scenes technical projects that distract them from their main objective of writing.

Tami has been an avid reader since childhood with a definite affinity for fairytales and short stories. Her constant belief in the seemingly unbelievable leads her to a passionate faith that everyone is uniquely sought and cherished by God, just as they are. This truth is soul-seared to her core because a loving God has picked her up, dusted her off, and forgiven her many flaws. She is acutely aware of all those she has failed and the undeserved grace He offers. Only through Him does her value exist, and somehow, He continues to love her so that she may love others. Her heart is for helping younger women see their true value and potential. Family is central to her life, and she adores spending time with her grandkids, who lovingly call her YuYa—a name that means "Love You." Most often you can find her camping with her husband Johnathan, enjoying time with her daughter and grandchildren or becoming hyper-fixated on a new hobby–always guided by her deep sense of curiosity and love.

Sources

1. **Quote:**
   "We are all just walking each other home."

   Citation:
   Ram Dass, *Be Here Now* (San Cristobal, NM: Lama Foundation, 1971).

2. **Quote:**
   "I may not jump in the ocean to drown with you, but you are welcome in my boat anytime."

   Citation:
   [Author's name omitted] (Personal communication).

3. **Quote:**
   "There is someone that I love even though I don't approve of what he does. There is someone I accept though some of his thoughts and actions revolt me. There is someone I forgive though he hurts the people I love the most. That person is... me."

   Citation:
   Often attributed to C.S. Lewis, but no verified source in his writings.

4. **Quote:**
   "Now if we are children, then we are heirs—heirs of God and co-heirs with Christ, if indeed we share in his sufferings in order that we may also share in his glory."

Citation:

Romans 8:17 (New International Version).

5. **Quote:**

"And so we know and rely on the love God has for us. God is love. Whoever lives in love lives in God, and God in them."

Citation:

1 John 4:16 (New International Version).

6. **Quote:**

"No man knows how bad he is till he has tried very hard to be good."

Citation:

C.S. Lewis, *Mere Christianity* (London: Geoffrey Bles, 1952).

7. **Quote:**

"and if children, then heirs—heirs of God and joint heirs with Christ, if indeed we suffer with Him, that we may also be glorified together."

Citation:

Romans 8:17 (New King James Version).

8. **Quote:**

"If you, then, though you are evil, know how to give good gifts to your children, how much more will your Father in heaven give good gifts to those who ask him!"

Citation:

Matthew 7:11 (New International Version).

9. **Quote:**

"But because of his great love for us, God, who is rich in mercy, made us alive with Christ even when we were dead in transgressions—it is by grace you have been saved."

Citation:

Ephesians 2:4–5 (New International Version).

10. **Quote:**

"And God raised us up with Christ and seated us with him in the heavenly realms in Christ Jesus, in order that in the coming ages he might show the incomparable riches of his grace, expressed in his kindness to us in Christ Jesus."

Citation:

Ephesians 2:6–7 (New International Version).

11. **Quote:**

"Be alert and of sober mind. Your enemy the devil prowls around like a roaring lion looking for someone to devour."

Citation:

1 Peter 5:8 (New International Version).

12. **Quote:**

"For the Lord gives wisdom; from his mouth come knowledge and understanding."

Citation:

Proverbs 2:6 (New International Version).

13. **Quote:**

"For our struggle is not against flesh and blood, but against the rulers, against the authorities, against the powers of this dark world and against the spiritual forces of evil in the heavenly realms."

Citation:

Ephesians 6:12 (New International Version).

14. **Quote:**

"You see, at just the right time, when we were still powerless, Christ died for the ungodly. Rarely will anyone die for a righteous person, though for a good person someone might possibly dare to die. But God demonstrates his own love for us in this: While we were still sinners, Christ died for us."

Citation:

Romans 5:6–8 (New International Version).

15. **Quote:**

"Finally, brothers and sisters, whatever is true, whatever is noble, whatever is right, whatever is pure, whatever is lovely, whatever is admirable—if anything is excellent or praiseworthy—think about such things."

Citation:

Philippians 4:8 (New International Version).

16. **Quote:**

"But the fruit of the Spirit is love, joy, peace, forbearance, kindness, goodness, faithfulness, gentleness and self-control. Against such things there is no law."

Citation:

Galatians 5:22–23 (New International Version).

17. **Quote:**

"You, dear children, are from God and have overcome them, because the one who is in you is greater than the one who is in the world."

Citation:

1 John 4:4 (New International Version).

18. Lupoff, Richard A. n.d. "*Groundhog Day* (film)." Wikipedia. Accessed August 28, 2024. https://en.wikipedia.org/wiki/Groundhog_Day_(film).

19. **Quote:**

"Dear friends, let us love one another, for love comes from God. Everyone who loves has been born of God and knows

God. Whoever does not love does not know God, because God is love. This is how God showed his love among us: He sent his one and only Son into the world that we might live through him. This is love: not that we loved God, but that he loved us and sent his Son as an atoning sacrifice for our sins. Dear friends, since God so loved us, we also ought to love one another. No one has ever seen God; but if we love one another, God lives in us and his love is made complete in us."

Citation:

1 John 4:7–12 (New International Version).

20. **Quote:**

"All shall be well, and all manner of thing shall be well."

Citation:

Julian of Norwich, *Revelations of Divine Love*, ca. 1395.

21. **Quote:**

"Forget the former things; do not dwell on the past. See, I am doing a new thing! Now it springs up; do you not perceive it? I am making a way in the wilderness and streams in the wasteland."

Citation:

Isaiah 43:18–19 (New International Version).

22. **Quote:**

"If I find in myself a desire which no experience in this world can satisfy, the most probable explanation is that I was made for another world."

Citation:

C.S. Lewis, *Mere Christianity* (London: Geoffrey Bles, 1952).

23. **Quote:**

"I have told you these things, so that in me you may have peace. In this world you will have trouble. But take heart! I have overcome the world."

Citation:

John 16:33 (New International Version).

24. **Quote:**

"So, the cross is always ready and waits for you everywhere. You cannot escape it no matter where you run, for wherever you go, you are burdened with yourself. Wherever you go, there you are."

Citation:

Thomas à Kempis, *The Imitation of Christ,* ca. 1440.

25. **Quote:**

"For I know that good itself does not dwell in me, that is, in my sinful nature. For I have the desire to do what is good, but I cannot carry it out. For I do not do the good I want to do, but the evil I do not want to do—this I keep on doing."

Citation:

Romans 7:18–19 (New International Version).

26. **Quote:**

"And you also were included in Christ when you heard the message of truth, the gospel of your salvation. When you believed, you were marked in him with a seal, the promised Holy Spirit, who is a deposit guaranteeing our inheritance until the redemption of those who are God's possession—to the praise of his glory."

Citation:

Ephesians 1:13–14 (New International Version).

27. **Quote:**

"I have been very zealous for the LORD God Almighty. The Israelites have rejected your covenant, torn down your altars, and put your prophets to death with the sword. I am the only one left, and now they are trying to kill me too." The LORD said, "Go out and stand on the mountain in the presence of the LORD, for the LORD is about to pass by." Then a great and powerful wind tore the mountains apart and shattered the rocks before the LORD, but the LORD was not in the wind. After the wind, there was an earthquake, but the LORD was not in the earthquake. After the earthquake came a fire, but the Lord was not in the fire. And after the fire came a gentle whisper. When Elijah heard it, he pulled his cloak over his face and went out and stood at the mouth of the cave. Then a voice said to him, "What are you doing here, Elijah?"

Citation:

1 Kings 19: 11-13 (New International Version).

28. **Quote:**

"When they saw him, they worshiped him; but some doubted. Then Jesus came to them and said, 'All authority in heaven and on earth has been given to me. Therefore go and make disciples of all nations, baptizing them in the name of the Father and of the Son and of the Holy Spirit, and teaching them to obey everything I have commanded you. And surely I am with you always, to the very end of the age.'"

Citation:

Matthew 28:17–20 (New International Version).